Crime and Punishment

Also by the author

DOSSIER: THE SECRET FILES THEY KEEP ON YOU

Crime and Punishment

A Radical Solution

ARYEH NEIER

STEIN AND DAY/*Publishers*/New York

Part of Chapter 2 appeared in somewhat different form in *The Civil Liberties Review*, Vol. II, no. 4, 1975.

First published in 1976
Copyright © 1975 and 1976 by Aryeh Neier
All rights reserved
Designed by David Miller
Printed in the United States of America
Stein and Day/*Publishers*/Scarborough House,
Briarcliff Manor, N.Y. 10510

Library of Congress Cataloging in Publication Data
Neier, Aryeh, 1937-
    Crime and punishment.
    1. Criminal law—United States. 2. Punishment—United States. I. Title.
KF9219. N4   345'.73   75-15743
ISBN 0-8128-1823-7

ACKNOWLEDGMENTS

Many of the proposals in this book grew out of conversations with friends and colleagues. Among those who helped me were Alvin Bronstein, Paul Chevigny, Leslie Dunbar, Joel Gora, Marilyn Haft, Trudy Hayden, Andrew Von Hirsch, Sheila Rothman, Herman Schwartz and Rena Uviller. I am very grateful to them for talks I enjoyed and for the stimulus they provided.

Ira Glasser and David Rothman read the manuscript prior to publication. They made many very perceptive suggestions and I owe them particular thanks. They should be absolved of blame for any deficiencies, however, since I did not follow all of their advice. I am also grateful for the skilled editorial guidance of Jeannette Hopkins.

My wife Yvette and my son David shaped their own lives to accommodate my writing of this book. As always, my greatest debt is to them.

ARYEH NEIER

Contents

Introduction

We deal with crime in strange ways.

A child who rapes is, after all, only a child. We let him out of prison after a few months. A child who is a truant from school or runs away from home is considered "incorrigible." He stays in prison much longer.

A man charged with a minor crime such as cashing a bad check faces a long period in prison if he insists he is innocent. The punishment is not for the crime. It is for the apparently more serious offense of putting everybody to the trouble of giving him a trial. If he committed armed robbery, he might not go to prison at all. He could accept a plea to a lesser charge, and his admission of guilt would probably be rewarded by quick release.

There are gun stores all over the United States. In most communities guns can be readily and openly purchased without special license. But the sale of marijuana is a serious crime all over the country. Mere possession of the drug for a person's own use remains a crime in all but a few states that have recently revised their laws. In their vigorous enforcement of the laws against possession of marijuana, police make close to half a million arrests a year.

Public drunkenness is the most serious part of our crime

problem. At least so it seems from the amount of time and effort police spend enforcing laws against it.

Everyone agrees recidivism is a great problem. It is conventional wisdom that prison gates are revolving doors. Yet we have thousands of laws prohibiting people with criminal records from getting jobs; we spend hundreds of millions of dollars on ever more efficient machinery for disseminating the records to public and private employers. Perhaps it is hoped the inability to obtain employment will help ex-convicts go straight. The effect is the opposite.

Thousands of people are killed and maimed annually by drunk drivers. Enforcement of the laws against driving under the influence of liquor is an important part of the duties of our police. Everybody agrees on that. But a recent upsurge in the number of arrests for drunk driving seems to have nothing to do with the actual incidence of this crime. Additional hundreds of thousands of people are suffering the pain and shame of arrest each year, apparently because the police have decided to use charges of drunk driving to give a veneer of legality to random searches of drivers and their cars.

This book contains a series of recommendations for revising public policy. It is written in the belief that the theories and practices governing the way we deal with crime do more to create the problem than to solve it. I offer some radical and some not so radical solutions, some of them novel and some of them not so novel.

My focus is limited to street crime. I have not concerned myself here with crimes by white-collar employees against the businesses that employ them, crimes by businesses against consumers, and crimes by government against us all. It is true, of course, that there is a great disparity between the way we treat the criminals who commit these crimes and the way we treat criminals who commit street crimes. Arrest, jail because of inability to make bail, a prison term, and punishment by record dissemination are not the penalties meted out to price fixers, polluters, and illegal wiretappers. But any comparison of their treatment with that accorded perpetrators of street crime is without much meaning to people frightened and injured by random violence to their persons and property.

Because of street crime, people stay out of public parks, stay home at night, move to the suburbs, close their schools and beaches to strangers, move across the country, and punish the cities by starving them. For people who are poor, private beaches, suburbs, and cross-country moves are no option. The poor, locked into the cities with the criminals, suffer the problems of the cities for the sins of the criminals, add multiple locks to their doors, and live in fear and trembling.

Political hard hats and racists have dominated public discussion of crime. They want to fight crime by "getting tough" with criminals, giving the police bigger sticks and guns, extending the power to search and seize, identifying and labeling children as potential criminals before they ever do anything wrong, tapping telephones, and bringing back the death penalty.

Liberals, radicals, and civil libertarians have fought back, usually ineffectually. They lack a program of their own for dealing with crime. They talk about racial and economic inequality. And while some part of the crime problem is surely rooted in those ills, not many people have the patience to wait until these ills are cured.

Redistribution of wealth and equality of the races have much to commend them quite aside from their impact on crime. A decade ago we were making some progress toward racial equality, if not redistribution of wealth. Since then, fear of crime has taken over and gotten in the way. The most effective government institution in the struggle for racial equality in the 1950s and 1960s was the Supreme Court of the United States. Because of fear of crime, the Court has been transformed. It is now a predictable ally of the hard hats in any matter affecting crime. The Supreme Court's role as a leader of efforts to bring about racial equality has been a casualty of the transformation.

There is no effect without a cause, as Voltaire's Dr. Pangloss would say. In the case of crime and racial inequality, however, the cause and the effect seem to me to have become intertwined. It may well be that we will have no peace in our streets until we solve the race problem. At the same time, as long as middle-class white Americans are terrified of the crimes committed by poor black Americans, they will not let them share their schools, neighborhoods, and jobs.

Since my proposals for dealing with crime do not deal with its economic causes, they are susceptible to the charge of superficiality. So be it. In my view, the surface wounds caused by crime must be bandaged before America will submit to the major surgery needed to remedy gross inequities in the opportunities afforded its citizens.

If I had faith in our capacity to spend our way out of the crime problem, I would not hesitate to recommend expenditures, even of enormous size. Almost any amount of money would be justified if it could heal ills that, according to a recent Gallup poll, have made nearly half of all Americans fearful of walking in their own neighborhoods after sundown. As it is, only a few of the remedies proposed in the pages that follow would require additional funds. The net effect of adopting all of the proposals offered would be a significant reduction in public spending.

Since 1968, the Federal Law Enforcement Assistance Administration has spent about $5 billion in grants to supplement the many billions of dollars already being spent on fighting crime by state and local governments and by the Federal government for its own law-enforcement apparatus. Even so, it is hard to find anyone who claims that the LEAA and its billions have eased the crime problem. There has certainly been no abatement in the growth of crime in the years the money was being spent. Many persons would share my view that the Federal government's efforts to combat crime with cash have been a disaster. The LEAA's dismal record only confirms my belief that we can fight crime more effectively if government does less rather than more. At times in these pages, I propose that government do less. Unless government has demonstrated its ability not to exacerbate a problem, I would prefer that it leave bad enough alone.

In making proposals I have deliberately, and rashly, erred on the side of assertiveness. Some of my colleagues in the American

Civil Liberties Union have expressed dismay over a few of my proposals, particularly those for punishment. They see them as excessively harsh. I, also, find my plan for very long prison sentences for certain kinds of violent crime is worrisome. The criticism from my associates has added to some of my earlier doubts about this proposal but has not persuaded me to withdraw it. I welcome reactions to all the proposals in the book and wish the logistics of book publication permitted some dialogue within its pages between an author and his critics. For now, I can only assure my critics—if assurance is needed—that I anticipate no headlong drive to follow my preaching. Before any of my proposals are adopted—if they are ever adopted—they will be debated long and hard. Most of them depart too radically from presently accepted methods of combating crime for it to be otherwise. There will be ample opportunity for critics to expose all deficiencies and demonstrate the error of my ways.

A major part of my purpose in writing this book is to help set in motion discussion of remedies for our crime problem by people who generally share my own commitment to civil liberties. The political hard hats have dominated the discussion because, with a few notable exceptions such as Norval Morris, dean of the University of Chicago School of Law, we civil libertarians have ceded it to them.

It should be clear I have been granted no license to speak on crime for civil libertarians generally or for the American Civil Liberties Union in particular. In some instances, the views I expound coincide with the policy positions of the ACLU, and many of the case histories I recount are drawn from court battles waged by the ACLU. In other areas covered in this book, the ACLU has no policy positions; in still others, my views diverge from the governing policy of the organization that employs me. Criticism of the ideas in this book is properly directed at me personally, not my employer.

This book is divided into two parts.

The first part, which deals with crime, offers proposals for redirecting the energies of law enforcement to make it more effective in combating crime. It also proposes changes in public policy aimed at mitigating the causes of crime.

I propose an end to arrests for consensual sexual relations, public drunkenness, marijuana, possession of narcotics, and offenses committed by children that would not be crimes if committed by adults. These categories of "crime" comprise half of all arrests. If they were eliminated, police, prosecutors, courts, and jails would be better able to cope with people who commit crimes of personal violence and crimes against property. (Such a change would also end the criminalizing of millions of citizens who might otherwise lead law-abiding lives. This is particularly important in the case of the hundreds of thousands of children arrested each year for status crimes. Public policy treats them as outlaws, and they become outlaws.

I propose to take away all guns from private citizens. If this could be done, violence would de-escalate sharply.

I propose changes in the management and employment practices of police departments intended to disrupt endemic police corruption. A decline in corruption would increase public respect for the police and would lead to greater citizen cooperation with the police.

I question a very rapidly developing new style of law enforcement that relies on random stops of more than 200,000 million citizens a day in the hope that a few—less than 1 percent—will be "hits" on a computerized system linking police all over the country with the FBI.

The causes of crime, I believe, often lie in family disruption, rootlessness, and transiency. There is much in American life that pulls families apart and keeps people on the move. But family disruption is greatly exacerbated by some public policies that serve no useful end. I propose changes in laws and practices that take children from their parents or keep them in the instability of long-term foster care. Giving each child the right to a permanent home seems to me an important way of preventing crime. I also propose changes in the policies of welfare departments, schools, and public housing agencies to reduce the family disruption caused by these bureaucracies.

The second part of this book deals with punishment. It proposes abandonment of those rationales for punishing people that are based on the assumption that punishment does them good. Punishment, in my view, rarely does any good for the person being punished. People should be punished when they deserve it, and then it should be done in a way that is both fair to them and beneficial to others.

This view of punishment leads me to propose a double standard in which "public crime" is punished differently from "private crime." I propose an end to plea bargaining because it blurs the distinction between guilt and innocence. I also propose a way of eliminating unfair disparities in sentencing.

For the most part, I reject alternatives to prison as a punishment for serious crime. Many of the possible alternatives seem to me worse than prison. I propose ways to make prisons better. I would eliminate parole entirely.

The most pervasive way of punishing people in America is to stigmatize them with criminal records. This is a punishment meted out to the innocent and guilty alike. I propose an end to punishment by stigma. It is more a cause of crime than an appropriate form of punishment.

PART ONE

Crime

1
The Crime of Sex

General enforcement of the sex laws would put the majority of Americans over fifteen years old in prison. But the laws are enforced with discrimination.

The vice division of the Los Angeles Police Department rented a suite on Sunset Boulevard and established offices for a fictitious corporation. The next step was a help-wanted advertisement in the weekly *Los Angeles Free Press:* "Sexy hostesses needed for gambling junkets. Entails foreign travel. Expenses paid." About 150 eager applicants showed up.

Fifty women were hired for the job. They were to depart on "junkets" to Las Vegas one week later, Christmas week, 1974. In the holiday spirit, there would be a party before departure at the Sheraton Universal Hotel.

At the party were twenty-five men looking for companions for trips to Las Vegas. As soon as the fifty women had arrived—surprise! They were all under arrest for prostitution. The twenty-five "gamblers" were undercover policemen.

The Los Angeles Police Department's elaborate caper was unusual. Ordinarily, the police entrap[1] women one at a time to arrest them for prostitution. An officer will strike up a conversation with a woman at a bar or on the street, arrange to go off to a hotel with her, and, somewhere along the way, identify himself as

19

a police officer and make an arrest. Sometimes the arrest takes place before any sexual act is performed, sometimes not.

Arrests for prostitution are a demonstration of sex discrimination. Almost all law enforcement is directed against women. Heterosexual activity by males is natural, even when promiscuous, but when women have many sex partners they are dirty. "From the standpoint of public health," an old California court decision said, "they are sometimes referred to as pestilential and their places of abode as pest houses."

Dragnet arrests are commonly used to supplement entrapment as a law-enforcement weapon against prostitution. Women picked up in dragnet arrests are charged with such lesser crimes as disorderly conduct or loitering for the purposes of prostitution. Sometimes the wrong people are swept up. A black woman arrested in Times Square in New York City a few years ago, nine months pregnant, had just emerged from a theater and was waiting for her husband to fetch the car from a garage. The police "pussy patrol" got to her first and hustled her off to the police station. Pointing out her obvious pregnancy didn't help. She was booked, and not until arraignment several hours later was she able to persuade anyone it was all a great mistake. The embarrassment of letting anyone know she could be mistaken for a prostitute made her decide not to file a suit against the police.

Dragnet arrests are still employed in the Times Square section of New York City, their purpose usually simple harassment. Women are held in station houses overnight and released in the morning. Charges are never filed, and no record of the arrests may ever exist.

The FBI says there were 55,800 reported arrests for prostitution in 1973, to take a recent year. These arrests take a great deal more time and effort by police than charges of loitering or disorderly conduct would require. Full-scale entrapment is usually necessary. It is virtually unheard of for anybody other than a police officer to swear out a complaint for prostitution. Males solicited by prostitutes are rarely so disturbed by the experience as to complain to the police and act as witnesses in court proceedings.

The males who become customers of prostitutes are seldom arrested. A 1975 decision by California Superior Court Judge Spurgeon Avakian stated:

In Oakland the woman is generally arrested and quarantined for a period of one to four days, and is tested for venereal disease and treated (if the test is positive) before being released on bail. The man is not detained. He is permitted to go his own way and at most given a citation which does not involve booking, fingerprinting, or bail, much less quarantine; nor does he attract the attention of the public or his family and friends which often attends the arrest and quarantine procedure.

Judge Avakian noted that the Oakland police conceded their discriminatory practice but offered several justifications. The female is a professional and a repeater, say the police, while the male makes a single contact and ceases such activity once cited. "No empirical data have been presented, and probably none exist because only the women seem to acquire 'rap sheets' in relation to prostitution," said the judge. "Moreover, this contention [that the male makes only a single contact] runs counter to the literature of the ages."

The police claim that the rate of venereal disease is higher among women prostitutes than their male customers was dismissed by Judge Avakian. "No comparison between customers and prostitutes is possible since the male customers are not quarantined and tested," he said, and furthermore, "venereal disease is communicated primarily by sexual intercourse, and both parties are equally exposed."

Police argue that giving prostitutes citations is impractical because they rarely carry identification. Judge Avakian responds that "citations are not used even if the woman has identification and is known to the police," and that "this is no reason why males should not be treated the same way as females . . . taking the male customers to jail for formal booking and all that goes with it would be a much greater deterrent than the citation procedure."

The Oakland police contend that the male customers are needed as witnesses against the female prostitutes. This "lays bare the sexual basis of the discrimination," said Judge Avakian. "Why should the man regularly occupy the favored role of being dubbed a necessary witness?" "The arrest and quarantine policy applies regardless of sex," the Oakland police told Judge Avakian. "Where a male drag queen is under surveillance in an area of prostitution and is found to be loitering, he is arrested and quarantined upon his violation of 647(b)." [2] The male customer of a prostitute gets a mild slap on the wrist. A male "drag queen" receives the same harsh treatment from the Oakland police as a woman prostitute.

Prostitutes have recently begun organizing to combat such unequal treatment. COYOTE, "a loose woman's organization" formed in the San Francisco Bay Area in 1973, is the pioneer. Named for what its founder and "chairmadam" Margo St. James says is the most promiscuous of animals, COYOTE is also an acronym for "Cast Off Your Old Tired Ethics." Ms. St. James is an energetic organizer with a sharp wit. She has inspired the creation of similar groups elsewhere. Hawaii's hookers have an organization known as DOLPHIN. New York City has PONY—"Prostitutes Of New York." Seattle has ASP—"Association of Seattle Prostitutes." These organizations have few members, yet, judging by the success of the gay rights movement in ending some of the worst police abuses—at least in large cosmopolitan cities—the development of organizations of prostitutes may be a necessary means of mitigating police harassment of the world's oldest profession.

Prostitution is now legal in most Western European countries. Solicitation and advertising are usually still crimes. Attitudes toward prostitution in the Scandinavian countries, England, France, and West Germany resemble the American attitude toward drunkenness. Unsightliness makes it criminal. If it is kept out of sight, no crime is committed.

In practice, if not in law, the United States seems to be moving in the same direction. Despite capers like the "sexy hostesses" advertisement the LAPD inserted in the *Los Angeles Free Press,* the police concentrate on visible prostitution. They devote considerable time and effort to arresting streetwalkers.

Hookers in bars get a lot less attention. Crackdowns against massage parlors usually come when advertising is too blatant or when they locate in neighborhoods that resent being sullied.

The essential vice of prostitution is unsightliness, disturbance of the aesthetic sensibilities of the passing pedestrian. Officials announcing a police crackdown against prostitution in New York City explicitly stated its direct connection to the Democratic party's decision to hold its 1976 presidential nominating convention in New York's Madison Square Garden. The timing of the drive against prostitution amounted to an admission that it is not the immorality of selling sex that is the essence of this crime. It is the visual pollution. Prostitutes on the street and bold advertisements for massage parlors offend the public relations image of the city.

In the "sexy hostesses" caper, the real target of the LAPD may have been the explicit advertising of sexual services that appears in profusion in each week's edition of the *Los Angeles Free Press*. A lively and intelligent periodical, the newspaper once tried to exclude sex advertising but found that it accounted for too much of the paper's revenue. Excluding advertisements for adult films, "live shows," "escort services," and massage parlors proved economically unfeasible. By entrapping women through an ad in the *Free Press* and arresting them as prostitutes, the LAPD might have been trying to deter such advertising. The mass arrests were certain to get a lot of attention and could intimidate readers of the *Free Press*'s sex ads. The women arrested as prostitutes may have been innocent victims in more ways than they suspected.

The police are busy pulling in prostitutes, entrapping them into commercial sex, devoting endless hours to what should never be a crime in the first place. Legalize prostitution. Ban public solicitation and anything other than discreet advertising, except possibly in designated red-light districts. Not that this would solve all problems—in a 1975 strike, French prostitutes occupied a prominent Catholic Church in Lyons for several days to protest police mistreatment. They claimed they could not earn enough unless they were allowed to entice customers on the street. The police were interfering with business enterprise. Even so, the management of prostitution in France, as in other countries of Western Europe, is far more civilized than it is in America, where public hypocrisy and sex discrimination turn the police into arbiters of private morality, a role they are ill-fitted to assume.

Repeal laws against prostitution and we will free large numbers of police to deal with serious crime. Empty the houses of detention for women and save public funds—nearly half the prisoners in these jails nationwide are there on charges of prostitution. Both steps would eliminate a major form of sex discrimination in the enforcement of the criminal laws. And they would help break the nexus between prostitution and more serious crime. They would give the police more manpower to hunt for real criminals.

The laws against prostitution help make prostitutes dependent on pimps. Pimps bail prostitutes out of jail and find them lawyers. Prostitutes also rely on pimps for private vengeance when they are injured by customers. The frequency with which customers injure prostitutes may be partly rooted in a belief that the woman who is herself breaking the law dares not seek police protection.

The criminal records acquired by prostitutes make it difficult for them to abandon the profession. Once she is branded with the stigma of an arrest for prostitution, a woman finds many other opportunities closed to her. Here, as elsewhere, arrests ensure recidivism instead of deterring it.

The Knapp Commission report on the New York City Police Department and the findings of other investigations demonstrate that prostitution is a major source of police corruption. Prostitution is a multibillion-dollar industry in the United States, and a fair portion of the profit winds up in little tin boxes and safe-deposit boxes kept by policemen. If there were no laws against prostitution, there would be no reason for people in the business to pay off police.

Prostitution helps finance organized crime, though it has largely been supplanted by the more lucrative trade in illegal drugs. Legalization of prostitution would eliminate its remaining utility as a rich source of revenue just as the end to Prohibition deprived organized crime of the source of income that really got it started in the United States.

Similar tactics of repression have been in common use against male homosexuals as against female prostitutes engaging in heterosexual acts. In many communities they are still in use, although the emergence of a gay rights movement has largely ended homosexual entrapment in cities like San Francisco and New York.

Before 1966, the New York City Police Department dressed its men in what they thought was homosexual garb (then more distinctive than now) and ordered them to frequent bars thought to be gathering places for homosexuals. The police would engage in conversations like those used to entrap prostitutes. When the practice was finally ended after it had become an embarrassing public issue, Sanford Garelik, chief inspector of the NYPD, announced a new assignment for the fifty vice squad plainclothesmen previously assigned to entrap homosexuals. They would be used to supplement enforcement of the laws against prostitution. In what must stand as a tribute to the versatility of New York City policemen, if not to the civil liberties sensibilities of their superiors, the very same officers who had spent their working hours obtaining solicitations from male homosexuals would switch to entrapping female prostitutes.

Blatant entrapment of homosexuals continues elsewhere. Eugene E., a resident of Jacksonville, North Carolina, and an openly professed gay, was selected as one target. Mr. E. ran the local adult bookstore and massage parlor. A police detective, as he later testified in court, was determined "to do something to run him [Mr. E.] out of town and get rid of him. He advised me himself he was gay." The detective drafted a seventeen-year-old Marine from nearby Camp LeJeune, a heterosexual, who had earned a few dollars by informing in drug cases for another Jacksonville police officer. This time he was to provide extra service. He was asked to complete a sex act with Eugene E. The

Marine did what he was told. In the privacy of his own home, Eugene E. performed fellatio on the Marine while the detective who sent the youngster on this assignment hid in some bushes across the street. The Marine came out of Mr. E.'s home and reported successful completion of the mission. Eugene E. was arrested and sentenced to a year in prison.

In more cosmopolitan cities, law enforcement against homosexuals focuses on sex acts in public, though the public nature of the acts is questionable.

Much furtive and anonymous homosexual activity takes place in parked cars. It occurs in "tearooms"—the rest rooms of homosexual bars and of public facilities that also serve other clienteles but have a reputation in the homosexual world as meeting places. Many homosexuals are married. Some still live with their parents. Some, who are in the closet, fear that their neighbors will discover their homosexual proclivities. They cannot go home to engage in homosexual acts. These quasi-public places are their only available facilities.

Police stationed at peepholes in rest rooms could be out watching for muggers in the parks. It was this sort of frivolous police activity that led to the arrest in 1967 of the late President Lyndon Johnson's aide, Walter Jenkins, in a YMCA basement. The "criminals" snared by the peephole police are often men like Jenkins, who was married and had six children. His homosexual life had to be relegated to places such as the YMCA basement where he was arrested. For such men the pain of exposure is often far greater than the pain of punishment meted out by a criminal court. Is the job of the police to punish such moral lapses?

Is a car a public or a private place? Heterosexual activity in parked cars is common. Until registering at a hotel or motel for an hour or two became accepted, use of cars was even more common. Many Americans had their first sexual experiences in cars. Police make little effort to enforce laws against such heterosexual activity. They discriminate against homosexuals. Kenneth C. is serving a fifteen-year sentence in an Oklahoma prison because he and another adult male were caught in an oral sex act one spring night in 1971. A policeman found Mr. C. and his friend in a car parked in a clump of bushes about a hundred yards from the nearest road.

It is often difficult for two males to register at a hotel or motel for a brief sexual encounter. For many, "tearooms" and parked cars must still suffice. And as long as homosexual sex retains that quasi-public character, police will have a rationale for enforcing laws against it.

Virtually all law enforcement against homosexuals is directed against males. There are few policewomen to entrap lesbians, though that is not the only reason. When men have sex with men, they are unnatural. "Thou shalt not lie down with mankind as with womankind," says the Bible, for "it is abomination." But religion, literature, and the courts have rarely concerned themselves with lesbianism. Lesbianism is only marginally relevant to an enforcement system preoccupied with masculinity and its prerogatives.

Prostitution is still illegal everywhere in the United States except for a few counties in Nevada, but eight states have repealed their consensual homosexual sodomy laws. The most recent repeal, in California, became effective in January 1976. In Colorado, Connecticut, Delaware, Hawaii, Illinois, Ohio, and Oregon, consensual homosexual sodomy is no longer a crime. In those states, homosexuals are arrested under statutes prohibiting lewd, indecent, or disorderly conduct in public places, but gays no longer need fear that sex acts with other adults committed in private will lead to arrest and prosecution. Police in those states do not spend valuable time entrapping gays into sex acts.

Consensual heterosexual sodomy among adults in private remains a crime in most states. The laws against it are infrequently enforced, but there are a few sad victims nonetheless. A husband and a wife in Virginia are both serving five-year prison sentences because their children found photographs of their parents engaged in oral sex and took them to school for show-and-tell. In punishing the sinning sodomists, the state of Virginia deprived the children of their parents, possibly an unspoken purpose of the long prison sentences.

Many states still have laws making adultery and fornication

crimes. A comprehensive revision of the penal law deleting the crime of adultery was adopted in New York State in 1966. Before the law could go into effect in 1967, the state legislature repaired the omission and restored the crime. There has been no reported prosecution for the crime of adultery in New York in this century. Most Americans at least have knowledge of adultery and fornication, even if they haven't committed those crimes themselves, but there is no outcry for enforcement of the laws against them. These practices are not especially linked with despised groups of people.

Sexual relations between people of the same sex, oral and anal relations between people of different sexes, purchased sex, sex between people married to others, and sex between unmarried people are all illegal in some states. A great many Americans commit one or more of these "crimes" on a regular basis.

Both prostitution and homosexuality are diminishing in significance as social problems. In the case of prostitution, this is partly because sex is plentifully available without payment. In metropolitan London in 1797, according to Patrick Colquhoun, a late-eighteenth-century British chronicler of crime, one Londoner in twenty was a prostitute. In the United States today, there may be 200,000 prostitutes, or one person in a thousand.

Today, also, there are more employment opportunities for women. In Dostoyevski's *Crime and Punishment*, the sensitive Sonya became a prostitute because she could find no other means to support her brothers and sisters. And, in the past, if prostitution was not the only employment available to a woman, it was often preferable to the alternatives. "The house in Brussels was real high class," Mrs. Warren informed her daughter in George Bernard Shaw's 1894 play about her "profession." It was "a much better place for a woman to be in than the factory where Anne Jane got poisoned. None of our girls were ever treated as I was treated in the scullery of that temperance place, or at the Waterloo bar, or at home. Would you have had me stay in them and become a worn-out old drudge before I was forty?"

Elimination of the criminal penalties for prostitution would not lead to more prostitution. Judging from the experience of other countries, legalization would not reverse the natural decline precipitated by market forces. Prostitution will always have a place in a free market economy, but it could well decline.

Homosexuality is also less of a social problem because it is more widely accepted today. Homosexuality is better understood and less feared than at any time since the days of the ancient Greeks. Fashions in theater, music, and clothing originating among homosexuals are now borrowed by others, apparently without discomfort. It seems only a matter of a decade or so before there will be a nationwide repeal of laws against consenting relations in private between adults of the same sex.

Elimination of the crimes of prostitution and consensual sodomy and maintenance of prohibitions on the most blatant forms of public solicitation would achieve the police purpose of limiting displays they—and we—find offensive. It would spare sexual minorities a great deal of pain. As for the efforts of government to enforce antiquated notions of public morality concerning private behavior, this is a peculiar way to use the police when they are urgently needed to protect the physical safety and the property of citizens. It is reminiscent of the deployment of the Berlin Schutzpolizei in the waning years of the Weimar Republic. Instead of dealing with rival bands of Nazis and Communists shooting up the streets, much of their time was spent on such matters as waging war against the sale of contraceptives from vending machines in men's rooms.

2

Public Boozers

Stanley M. was arrested a few blocks from West Madison Street, Chicago's skid row, on an unseasonably warm day in May 1973. In the station lockup, police asked how often he had been arrested. He didn't know exactly, but it had been more than 200 times. The police had records of only 168 arrests but conceded that Mr. M. was probably right.

Stanley M.'s crime was public drunkenness. His arrest that day was one of about 2.25 million arrests for drunkenness in 1973, about 25 percent of all arrests for all crimes, a typical year's record. Because there is a much higher rate of convictions for drunkenness than for any other crime, about 35 percent of all convictions that year were for public drunkenness.[1]

I propose that we abolish public drunkenness as a crime. If we did so, we could free the police to handle serious crimes.

It is not possible to find anyone with any enthusiasm for these arrests. Certainly not Stanley M. He was locked in a cell with twelve other men in stifling heat of close to 100 degrees. They were fed only bologna sandwiches. Their bath was a hosing down. And that day was better than some others. Nobody vomited or urinated on anybody else, and no fights broke out.

The police who arrested Stanley M. share his lack of enthusiasm. They hate the sight and the stench of drunks. In cities

30

where police must go to court on their own time after finishing duty, they particularly begrudge the time they waste on poor souls like Stanley M.

Not even government officials who seek to portray themselves as guardians of public morality can bring themselves to champion drunk arrests. "We have to find ways to clear the courts of the endless stream of 'victimless crimes' that get in the way of serious consideration of serious crimes," former President Richard Nixon told the National Conference on the Judiciary in March 1971. "There are more important matters for highly skilled judges and prosecutors than minor traffic offenses, loitering and drunkenness."

Question: Then who does want drunks arrested? Answer: That amorphous entity, the general public. Question: Why? Answer: They are unsightly. We don't want to look at them. Question: Do arrests serve this purpose? Answer: Yes. When drunks stray out of the skid row areas to which we confine them, they are almost sure to get arrested.

Not all drunks get arrested, however. A middle-class citizen who has one or more too many will often be helped home by a solicitous policeman. The great majority of all arrests for drunkenness involve fewer than 200,000 derelicts. They get arrested over and over again. At any given moment 35,000 or so are in jail. The rest are out on the streets between periods in jail.

In the spring of 1964, lawyers practicing in the lower criminal courts in New York City began to notice that the derelicts who had previously received five- and ten-day jail sentences were being confined for the maximum time allowable under the disorderly-conduct law then in effect in the state: six months behind bars. The New York World's Fair was about to open, and the city's leading "power broker," Robert Moses, was president of the Fair. Moses had apparently passed the word to police, prosecutors, and judges that he wanted derelicts in the city's midtown areas arrested and locked up until the World's Fair shut down for the winter. He didn't want journalists and tourists to see any derelicts. Moses hid them away in the jails the way

Potemkin hid the Russian serfs behind the façades of the villages he constructed to deceive Catherine II into thinking all was well in her empire. As part of its campaign to persuade the Democrats to hold their 1976 presidential nominating convention in New York City, the police pledged to keep the convention area free of "undesirables." Fortunately for the drunks, the convention only lasts a week or so.

Police do not as a general practice give such unfortunates breath tests or blood tests to determine if they are really drunk. Tests are administered to drivers suspected of being under the influence because it really matters whether they are drunk. It doesn't really matter whether persons arrested for "public drunkenness" are drunk. The key word in this crime is *public*. The ugliness of the display is what matters. It offends us to see derelicts, whether or not they are actually drunk. But if one of the country's many millions of middle-class alcoholics is on the street, chances are he won't be arrested. He may be more drunk than the derelict but not nearly so unsightly. The drunken derelict is usually dirty, disheveled. He may be lying on the street or in the gutter.

The police say they help the derelict, provide a kind of social work. The derelicts swept up by the police may suffer from disease. Still, medical treatment of drunks in jail is rare. Confined in close quarters, any who are not ill may catch a disease from others. Also, police tend to avoid arresting the derelicts who are in the worst shape. It is so difficult and messy to process them through the courts. When merchants and neighborhood residents complain, police will sometimes put a drunk in a car and unload him in a deserted neighborhood. Years ago, civic officials in small towns would put drunks on trains and buses headed for the nearest big city. Out of sight, out of mind.

Public drunkenness has been a crime since at least 1606 when it was prohibited in England by an Act of Parliament. It has been a crime throughout American history, is a crime in almost every American state and in almost every country in the world. The laws against it have made no difference in suppressing drunkenness. The way the laws are enforced simply helps determine which neighborhoods are afflicted and which are protected.

In 1968, the United States Supreme Court considered a challenge to the constitutionality of the laws against public drunkenness. Leroy Powell, a chronic alcoholic, had been arrested many times and testified he was unable to stop drinking. The Supreme Court pondered whether it was wrong to punish a person for conduct he could not control. Six years earlier the Court had ruled in *Robinson* v. *California* that the state could not punish a person for the crime of being addicted to the use of narcotics. It was cruel and unusual punishment, it said, to punish someone for a disease. Could that earlier ruling apply here? No, said Justice Thurgood Marshall, on behalf of the Supreme Court. Powell, Marshall wrote,

was convicted, not for being a chronic alcoholic, but for being in public while drunk on a particular occasion. The State of Texas thus has not sought to punish a mere status, as California did in *Robinson;* nor has it attempted to regulate [Powell's] behavior in the privacy of his own home. Rather, it has imposed upon [Powell] a criminal sanction for public behavior which may create substantial health and safety hazards, both for [Powell] and for members of the general public, and which offends the moral and esthetic sensibilities of a large segment of the community. This seems a far cry from convicting one for being an addict, being a chronic alcoholic, being mentally ill or a leper.

Powell presented no health and safety hazards. The sight of his offense should not have outraged the moral sensibilities of Texans. Still, Justice Marshall stated that Powell's drunkenness "offends the ... esthetic sensibilities." Powell, I believe, *was* guilty of a status crime: the crime of offending aesthetic sensibilities, or, more succinctly, *the crime of unsightliness.*

To show the discrepancy between legal standards of the sort envisioned by the United States Constitution and the ordinary procedures for prosecuting derelicts, the New York City Legal Aid

Society assigned attorneys to defend them vigorously for a brief period in 1966. The conviction rate plunged from 98 percent to 2 percent! The system for processing derelicts in most American cities can work only as long as judges, prosecutors, police, and defense attorneys abide by a spoken or unspoken agreement to ignore constitutional standards.

Derelicts bring out the worst in police. Police think of them as a lower species of life. When derelicts stumble and fall as they are being arrested, police may kick and shove them along. Who would believe the complaints of a derelict? Derelicts are often too far gone to pay appropriate obeisance to police authority, and the disobedient may encounter police brutality. Every study of the subject has demonstrated that most police abuse comes from defiance of their authority.

Derelicts also encourage police to lie. For purposes of convenience, a single officer will be designated as the arresting officer for a group of derelicts, whether or not he made the arrests. This spares the policeman's friends, the real arresting officers, the trouble of hanging around the court until their cases are reached. Officers may therefore testify under oath about conduct they did not actually see, a tactic adapted for use in another mass arrest situation: antiwar demonstrations. Used by the District of Columbia police at the time of the 1971 "Mayday" arrests, it led to a vigorous court dispute and to the subsequent dismissal by the courts of all charges against the demonstrators. But these were middle-class protesters. They were listened to.

There are some experiments in treating drunkenness in public places as a disease not a crime. Several cities have established detoxification centers. They imitate programs in countries like Poland, which requires that cities of more than 100,000 population set up public drying-out stations. In the United States, St. Louis established the first detoxification center in 1966.

The St. Louis system is called "voluntary." In practice, however, it isn't. A drunk or derelict picked up by the police is given the choice of entering the detoxification center or of facing criminal prosecution. Only persons brought in by the police may enter the detoxification program. Those who elect it stay for five to seven days. Each "patient" gets a medical examination, and if seriously ill from some cause other than acute intoxication, he is transferred to a local hospital or health center, an American Bar Foundation report says. "The patient is showered, perhaps deloused, and then assigned to a bed. Patients remain in bed for one or two days, receiving vitamins, forced fluids, tranquilizers, and a high protein diet . . . the patient is urged to participate in physical therapy and is included in an inpatient therapy program which includes sociodrama, group therapy, and didactic lectures." [2]

In its early days, the St. Louis system had the enthusiastic cooperation of the police. The professional staff at the detoxification center went out of its way to make the police comfortable as they walked the drunks through the admission process. The police were proud of participation in a rehabilitation program.

Police enchantment has disappeared. The center was moved to a less convenient spot, and the new staff provided fewer courtesies to the police. The center's effectiveness proved to have been oversold. Like the drunk tanks in the city's jail, the detoxification center began to seem like a revolving door, and reports of police brutality, which had virtually ended in the early days of the center, began to reappear.

In New York City in November 1967, a private organization, the Vera Foundation, with the financial support of a grant from the Ford Foundation, set up a voluntary detoxification program. Its claims are modest, but it has had some success.[3]

In the Vera Foundation program, recovered alcoholics operate in the Bowery, New York's principal skid row area, with plainclothes police officers in rescue teams. The recovered alcoholic talks to each derelict in distress, and offers the opportunity to visit the detoxification center. The police officer waits in a car, and if medical attention is needed, summons an ambulance. No threat of arrest is made. The derelict can reject the offer of assistance. If he accepts, he is free to change his mind and leave the treatment program at any time.

In the detoxification center, the derelict is screened by a doctor, showered and deloused, and sent to bed. He gets a complete physical examination and appropriate medication. Most of the patients are walking around after twenty-four hours. After the third day, the patient sees a caseworker and discusses what to do next. If the patient is willing to try to return to normal life, he is referred to one of about twenty-five aftercare programs. Three in four derelicts approached on the streets of the Bowery accept the offer.

Most of the Bowery derelicts the rescue teams pick up have been drinkers for one or two decades. Most drink wine and support themselves with occasional spot jobs or by panhandling. "The project has confirmed that 'rehabilitation' for many Bowery men cannot be measured in conventional terms such as permanent sobriety, holding steady jobs, acquiring property, and establishing families, and other social ties," says a Vera report. "On the other hand, deteriorated men can be motivated to make some changes in their lives, and while such changes may seem small, they can be extremely significant to each man and the community that must deal with him. A derelict can lengthen his average time between drinking sprees from a few weeks to months. He can obtain better paying jobs for longer periods of time. He can make better use of the city's health resources and obtain regular medical and dental attention. He can, through use of medically prescribed tranquilizers and other drugs, combat periods of stress by means other than alcohol." [4]

Nor are police needed even as partners on the rescue team. Civilian rescue teams are unlikely to be as preoccupied with their authority as police patrols and therefore are unlikely to respond so brutally when they sense defiance. And even if a program is labeled "voluntary," the visible participation of police inevitably adds a coercive element. Legal theorist Herbert Packer argued, "If compulsion is applied, social service becomes a tyranny both subtler and more coercive than the criminal sanction." [5] I agree.

A cynical argument is advanced, however, in favor of police-run programs like the one in St. Louis. The Vera Foundation's minimal use of police might be better, most readily concede, but, it is said, the country's priorities being what they are, Federal money is available to finance law-enforcement programs. No police control, no money.

But we need to free police from such onerous chores so that they can deal with serious crime. And there should be money available to stop muggings and burglaries. Police are not really needed even to bring derelicts to detoxification centers. If public drunkenness were wiped off the books as a crime, police could save the endless hours spent booking their charges and hanging around courts to testify against them. They could get about their real business—to make the streets *safe*, not to make them *sightly*. Public drunkenness is usually a matter of health and sanitation, not of crime.

Packer thought arrests for public drunkenness could be stopped whether or not detoxification facilities were available. Such arrests should end as a matter of principle. The status of unsightliness should not be a crime.

As a practical matter, the Supreme Court's decision in the *Powell* case still stands in the way of a cessation of arrests for public drunkenness in the absence of an alternative way of removing unsightly people from the "better" streets and parks when they stray from skid row areas.

Proposals to deal with the problem of alcoholism through changes in the laws governing the advertising and sale of liquor are folly, as our experience with Prohibition and the efforts of other countries to limit the sale of alcohol should persuade us. Sparsely populated Finland, with especially severe limits on the sale of alcohol, averages about 150,000 arrests annually for public drunkenness—between two and three times the rate for the United States. After a period of prohibition about as long as the United States experiment—it was ended by an overwhelming popular referendum vote—Finland went back to the status quo. Since then, the Finns have barred all liquor advertising, limited sales of packaged liquor to a relatively small number of government-operated *alko* stores, and licensed the sale of hard liquor by the drink, mostly in establishments where the customer is also required to purchase a meal. Except in a handful of fairly expensive hotels and nightclubs, it is not possible to purchase anything stronger than a medium-alcohol-content beer in Finland without eating. The ubiquitous Finnish *baari* sells weak beer (only 3.2 percent alcohol) and fruit juices. Yet any visitor to Finland observes much public drunkenness.

Fortunately for the Finns, their police must contend with very little serious crime and can devote themselves to arresting drunks without leaving the citizenry unprotected. Not so in the United States. Here, to treat public drunkenness as a crime is a waste of money and a danger to society. It gives real criminals more leeway.

In the United States, we need a federally financed program of voluntary detoxification centers like the Vera Foundation's Bowery project—but, even better, without any role for police at all, not even the subordinate part Vera assigns to the plainclothes officer who waits in the car. To use recovered alcoholics, as the Bowery project does, is a useful and productive idea. It provides jobs for people who have trouble getting jobs, and it puts on rescue teams individuals who know the problem firsthand.

Provide an alternative to the use of police for sanitation work—removal of unsightly people from the streets. Give these victims emergency medical attention. Provide the opportunity for rehabilitation for the occasional derelict who will accept it. Most important, rewrite the laws so that public drunkenness is no longer a crime at all. Where there is no crime there is no need for punishment and the expensive, time-consuming process of arrest, conviction, and imprisonment.

3
Private Smokers

Almost half the population between eighteen and thirty have probably committed the crime of smoking, possessing, or selling a marijuana cigarette.

Several years ago, the San Francisco Police Crime Laboratory estimated it spent 38 percent of its time analyzing marijuana. Since then, the number of arrests for marijuana has tripled. At a conservative estimate, police laboratories now spend 50 percent of their time trying to determine whether seeds, stems, and leaves that police have seized are really marijuana or only oregano. The police could use that time to investigate crime.

An artist living in a rural area of upstate New York was approached by a man who said he was a purchasing agent for the Cunard Line. The agent had seen a painting by the artist at an exhibit. Did the artist, by any chance, have on hand a supply of paintings? Cunard would be interested in purchasing them to decorate the public rooms on one of its ships.

The artist was delighted. He had a more than adequate supply on hand. By this deal he could make more money than he had earned in his entire career as a painter.

39

The customer visited the artist's home to inspect the paintings. He was enthusiastic. One thing remained to clinch the deal. The purchasing agent's boss would also have to see the paintings. A time was arranged. Several days before the appointment, the artist got a phone call from the purchasing agent. Just one more thing. Could the artist come up with some marijuana for his boss? That would ensure everything went smoothly. With some reluctance, the artist agreed.

On the appointed day, the purchasing agent and his boss arrived. The marijuana changed hands. As soon as the transaction was completed, the two people who said they were from Cunard revealed their true identities: They were narcotics detectives, and the artist was under arrest. As far as I know, no one bothered to consult the Cunard firm about this appropriation of the company's name.

The phony Cunard agents were somewhat more scrupulous than a Vermont policeman, Paul D. Lawrence. He had an outstanding record: 600 drug convictions in six years. That was until March 1975, when Francis Murray, the prosecutor of Chittenden County, wrote to Governor Thomas Salmon, asking him to pardon all 600 of those convicted on Lawrence's testimony. It seems Lawrence had a habit of planting the evidence—marijuana, cocaine, or heroin—on anyone he suspected of drug use. One girl testified at a trial that Lawrence picked her up while she was hitchhiking. After she turned down his invitation to spend the night with him, so her testimony went, he arrested her for selling him drugs.

Motorists are victims of a great many of the close to half a million marijuana arrests each year—420,700 in 1973, according to the FBI. The number has been rising sharply year by year and may be more than half a million by now. It is standard practice for police to testify that they spotted marijuana in the possession of drivers stopped on traffic charges. Typically, a police officer testifies that the marijuana was on the seat next to the driver, or fell out of a hip pocket when the driver reached for his license, or was visible in the glove compartment when the driver reached in there to get his license. Since the marijuana was in plain view, according to this testimony, no illegal search was made.

The newest fad in police testimony on marijuana is for the officer to state he smelled a strong odor of marijuana smoke when he stopped the car. This gives the officer probable cause to believe a crime is taking place. He then searches the car and its passengers. If he finds marijuana, he can then make a legal arrest. Linda McCartney, wife of ex-Beatle Paul McCartney, was arrested by a Los Angeles police officer with a good sense of smell who said he detected the odor of marijuana smoke in the car she was driving. She was convicted.

Partygoers sometimes get arrested in large numbers for marijuana possession. Again, it is the odor of marijuana smoke, or the subsequent claim of the odor, that is used to establish probable cause for searches. It works like this. A policeman rings a doorbell and announces that a neighbor has complained about noise at the party. As the officer is talking to the host at the door, he smells the marijuana, a group of officers enter, they search, and the arrests take place. One tip-off about the choreography for these arrests is the presence of a large group of police accompanying the officer who comes to ask for a decrease in the noise level.

Rock concerts are another favorite target. When the British group Pink Floyd staged a five-night concert in Los Angeles in April 1975, the LAPD responded to the challenge. Chief Ed Davis, whose police must cope with crime in one of the most violent cities in the nation, was able, nevertheless, to deploy a large force to catch anybody smoking marijuana while listening to Pink Floyd. There were 511 arrests made, mostly for possession of marijuana. At that, Davis wasn't satisfied. He complained that 70 percent of the people who filled the Sports Arena were smoking marijuana. Apparently, he would have liked to arrest them all.

Until just a few years ago, fifty-year sentences for marijuana possession were fairly common. In Michigan, a poet received a forty-year sentence for giving two marijuana cigarettes to two undercover police who spent months cultivating his friendship before they were able to arrest him for "possession" and "dispensing." On appeal, the sentence was overturned on constitutional grounds. He had already served three years. In Ohio, a young couple sold five dollars' worth of marijuana to a neighbor. A judge sentenced them to twenty to forty years in prison as a lesson for others.

Until August 1973, when a new law went into effect, Texas enjoyed the dubious distinction of imposing the most cruel punishments on marijuana users. The new law, reducing the crime of possession to a misdemeanor punishable by a maximum jail sentence of six months, did not have any retroactive impact on users of marijuana sentenced under the old Texas law. Eight hundred persons remained in Texas prisons, serving average sentences of nine and a half years. Thirteen of these were in for life. In some instances they were victims of deliberate entrapment of political activists. Lee Otis Johnson, a young black who had been a leader of the Student Non-Violent Coordinating Committee (SNCC), was one of the entrapped. Until his conviction was overturned because prejudicial publicity had deprived him of a fair trial, Johnson was serving a thirty-year sentence for passing a marijuana joint to an undercover agent.

Some of the victims of the old Texas law have now completed their sentences, and others have had their sentences commuted by the Texas Board of Pardons and Parole. Even so, many persons are still serving out sentences in Texas prisons for marijuana crimes committed before the Texas legislature saw fit to abandon thirty- and forty-year sentences.

In his account of the Persian Wars written in the fifth century B.C., Herodotus said that marijuana was popular among the Scythians, a nomadic people who inhabited the Eurasian steppes and who are remembered today chiefly for the magnificent gold objects they left behind.

Hemp grows in Scythia: it is very like flax; only that it is a much coarser and taller plant: some grows wild about the country, some is produced by cultivation [the Greek historian reported]. The Scythians ... take some of this hempseed, and, creeping under the felt coverings, throw it upon the red-hot stones; immediately it smokes, and gives out such a vapor as no Grecian vapor-bath can exceed. The Scyths, delighted, shout for joy, and this vapor serves them instead of a water-bath; for they never by any chance wash their bodies with water.[1]

Marijuana became a dangerous drug to be banished by means of severe criminal penalties in the early part of the twentieth century. It was a period of intense racial xenophobia. "Cocaine raised the specter of the wild Negro, opium the devious Chinese," David Musto has pointed out in his excellent history of American drug policies. As for marijuana, "Chicanos in the Southwest were believed to be incited to violence by smoking" it.[2] Criminal laws to control these feared groups were thought essential to prevent them from corrupting the white race.

The first state antimarijuana law was adopted in Utah in 1915, about the time that large-scale immigration from Mexico got under way. Immigration across the border, legal and illegal, continued to be heavy throughout the 1920s. By the end of that decade, sixteen Western states had adopted antimarijuana laws. Hostility to Mexicans increased during the 1930s as the Depression put them into competition with whites for scarce jobs. "Patriotic" societies were formed to restrict immigration and suppress the evils Mexicans were thought to be introducing into American society. Marijuana became a natural focus of attacks by the patriotic societies, and their efforts culminated in 1937, the year following the distribution of the scare movie *Reefer Madness*. Marijuana was outlawed by the federal government except for use in birdseed, where it could be used if first sterilized.

Marijuana is no longer popularly associated with Mexicans. In the 1960s, young people made it a symbol of their rejection of the life-styles of business America. In a February 1973 report to the President, the National Commission on Marijuana and Drug

Abuse reported that its surveys showed that some 26 million Americans had tried marijuana at least once and that at least 13 million were current users. By now, those numbers must have grown substantially. It seems likely that a majority of the population between eighteen and thirty has smoked marijuana. In doing so, almost all of them committed crimes.

It is no longer a crime to possess one ounce or less of marijuana in Oregon. In October 1973, a state law took effect making possession of small quantities of the drug a civil offense with a maximum fine of $100. A year later, the Drug Abuse Council surveyed the state to discover what changes in marijuana usage had occurred during that year.[3] The survey demonstrated that while there were no significant changes in the number of people using the drug, those using it were doing so less. Among users, 40 percent said they had cut down on their usage; only 5 percent said they were using marijuana more often. The rest reported no change in their habits. Among those in the Oregon survey whose use of marijuana declined in the first year after abolition of criminal penalties, the principal reason given was "no interest" in the drug.

Other states are not rushing to repeal their laws making possession of marijuana a crime; still, Oregon's experience has helped persuade several state legislatures to do so. Maine, Colorado, Alaska, Ohio, and California enacted laws similar to Oregon's in 1975 to go into effect in 1976. Drives to pass similar laws elsewhere fell short of success in the 1974 and 1975 sessions of many state legislatures.

By any rational standards, repeal of criminal penalties for marijuana possession should be sweeping the state legislatures. Public opinion has shifted rapidly in favor of eliminating criminal penalties. A presidential commission, the American Bar Association, the Governing Board of the American Medical Association, the National Council of Churches, and the American Public Health Association all favor elimination of criminal penalties. There is little organized opinion on the other side. Even such conservative spokesmen as William F. Buckley, Jr., who says he sampled marijuana on a boat beyond American territorial waters to avoid violating the law, have endorsed efforts to stop making possession of marijuana a crime.

True, the old arguments against marijuana are still rehearsed in state legislative debates. It produces sexual promiscuity. It makes people violent. It leads to heroin. It is dangerous to health.

Except for the concern about health, these are more interesting as historical curiosities than as serious arguments. The claim that marijuana makes people violent, for example, seems largely founded on etymology. The sometime philologist Harry Anslinger, better known as the hard-line and long-time commissioner of the Federal Bureau of Narcotics,[4] popularized the view that the word *assassin* derives from the name given to an eleventh-century Persian military order noted for cruelty, barbarity, and murder. They were users of hashish (which is, like marijuana, a derivative of cannabis), hence the name "Assassins."

Anslinger and his Bureau of Narcotics were also the source of a good deal of prurient literature portraying marijuana as a sexual stimulant. If a brutal sex crime was committed and any traces of marijuana were found in the possession of the criminal or the victim, Anslinger announced that the drug was the cause of the crime. Bureau publications were jammed with stories notable for their lurid detail, even if remarkably deficient in any efforts to prove a cause-and-effect relationship between marijuana, sex, and crime.

The theory that marijuana is a steppingstone to heroin was also popularized by Anslinger and his associates in the Bureau of Narcotics. By the 1950s, this was the Bureau's principal argument against marijuana. Indeed, at the time, there was some statistical correlation between the users of the two drugs. Both drugs were then principally used in black ghettos. More recently, however, marijuana use has spread throughout American society. Heroin has not followed it. There are apparently no pharmacological connections between the drugs, and no physiological reasons for users of the one to turn to the other. If they are linked at all, it is by the criminal laws making possession of either drug illegal.

It is alleged that marijuana use leads to other dangerous drugs: hallucinogens, cocaine, and the amphetamines. Again, there appears to be no link except those forged by the criminal law. As long as marijuana is illegal, it must be purchased from people who traffic in illegal drugs. Thus purchasers come in contact with individuals who may be purveying other drugs and who may urge them upon their customers. Once a person puts himself outside the law through use of one illegal drug, it is not so large a step to another illegal drug. Finally, the evident foolishness of the treatment of marijuana by the law may delude users into assuming that the dangers of other drugs are equally mythical.

Claims that marijuana is damaging to health must be taken more seriously. There are studies purportedly showing that marijuana damages the brain, lowers the body's resistance to cancer and other diseases, increases the chances of birth defects, and leads to sterility and impotence in men. The supporting evidence is slender, and much of it is speculative. "Some researchers are drawing conclusions about the harm from marijuana which far exceed the data presently available," according to Dr. Thomas E. Bryant, president of the Drug Abuse Council. "In some cases, the researchers themselves appear to have set out to support a preconceived notion. The result has been a series of reports, some of which resemble propaganda more nearly than scientific research." [5] The Consumers Union reached a similar conclusion.

Out of all these many studies [Edward M. Brecher writes in the March 1975 *Consumer Reports*], a general pattern is beginning to emerge. When a research finding can be readily checked—either by repeating the experiment or devising a better one—an allegation of adverse marijuana effects is relatively short-lived. No damage is found—and after a time the allegation is dropped (often to be replaced by allegations of some other kind of damage due to marijuana).

Despite the lack of substantial evidence on the dangers to health from marijuana it can hardly be asserted that the drug is harmless. But it has not been shown to be comparably dangerous to nicotine and alcohol, drugs in common use that do not presently draw criminal penalties on their users.

The absence of rational reasons for preserving criminal statutes to punish marijuana users makes it necessary to inquire into the possible motives of those resisting change. Leaving aside inertia, the answer seems to be that in the last decade marijuana laws have served the same purpose as when they were first enacted. They are a social control device for use against undesirables.

In the second half of the 1960s, marijuana became the drug of choice for American *Wandervogel,* youths in revolt both against the business ethic of the men in gray-flannel suits with gray-flannel minds and against the power ethic that produced the war in Vietnam. In turn, the marijuana laws became a major weapon for use in a counterattack against the young rebels. A Jerry Rubin might be nailed on marijuana charges even if the appellate courts overturned his convictions in demonstration cases. In rejecting marijuana and marijuana users, people could demonstrate their own political sentiments. In the words of a country music song:

> We don't smoke marijuana in Muskogee,
> We don't take our trips on LSD,
> We don't burn our draft cards down on Main Street,
> 'Cause we like living right and free.

As young people all over the nation supplanted Chicanos in the Southwest and blacks in urban ghettos as the principal users of marijuana, arrest rates soared. The new users of marijuana were no more hated than those earlier users, but there were so many more of them and their use of the drug was so much more visible. In 1965, there were only 18,815 marijuana arrests nationwide. By 1970, the number had multiplied tenfold to 188,682. In 1971, there were 215,828 marijuana arrests; in 1972, there were 292,179 marijuana arrests; and by 1973, the last year for which figures are available at this writing, 420,700. It is not evident that the increasing numbers of arrests increased public safety.

Marijuana laws have provided police with a weapon to harass and punish their "hippie" enemies. Arrests of young people for marijuana offenses have earned police the enmity of a significant part of the generation that came to maturity in the 1960s. Hundreds of thousands of young people have been made outlaws. According to the National Commission on Marijuana and Drug Abuse, 81 percent of those arrested for marijuana offenses were never previously convicted of any crime.

In reporting marijuana arrests to prospective employers and licensing agencies, it is standard practice for law-enforcement agencies to identify the charge as a "narcotic drug arrest." It may be that this reporting, which exacerbates the injury done by the arrest, is simply a legacy of an earlier time when it was thought marijuana had the addictive effect of a narcotic. Or it may reflect the police mentality as revealed in a story Alexander Solzhenitsyn tells. In *The Gulag Archipelago,* the Russian writer describes the case of a man sentenced to prison for ten years for stealing a spool of thread. In the official documents, this man's crime became stealing "200 meters of sewing material."

Marijuana arrests account for more than 5 percent of all arrests for all crimes. They cost a great deal of time and money that could be better devoted to dealing with serious crime. When the police respond to a report of a prowler forty minutes after a call has been made and too late to prevent a robbery or rape, it may be because another officer who could have responded sooner was busy arresting a long-haired youth on marijuana charges. The waste in police resources is particularly great in the use of crime laboratories where drugs are analyzed. "One of the principal causes of the failure of crime labs to provide adequate service in other major crime cases can be charged to the epidemic of cases involving illegal drugs and the abuse of legal drugs," says police scientist Jay Cameron Hall. "If the police were freed from the frenetic and often stupid pursuit of the modern marijuana user," the former director of the Pasadena Crime Laboratory continues, "the crime labs would automatically feel a relief in the case load." 6

The high cost of enforcing marijuana laws will not spur many state legislatures to repeal criminal sanctions. If repeal begins to sweep the country, it will be because marijuana is no longer identified with a hated class. The hippie subculture is fast disappearing, but marijuana use remains widespread and may be growing. If and when marijuana users become indistinguishable from everyone else, criminal penalties will lose their charm for those intent on their use as a social control device. After a lag of two or three years while it sinks in that marijuana is no longer the drug of a rebel subculture, most state legislatures will get rid of their laws making marijuana use a crime.

A May 1975 decision by the Alaska Supreme Court provides another method of changing the marijuana laws. The five judges of that court were unanimous in overturning the state's law against marijuana possession as a violation of the Alaska constitution's guarantee of the right to privacy. Earlier, courts in several other states had rejected similar arguments. The Alaska judges, however, wrote with some pride of the special character of life in their state as the reason for a broader protection of privacy than has yet been recognized by courts elsewhere. "Our territory and now state," said the Alaska Supreme Court, "has traditionally been the home of people who prize their individuality and who have chosen to settle or to continue living here in order to achieve a measure of control over their own lifestyles which is now virtually unattainable in many of our sister states."

It would be a mistake to rely on the courts to rid us of the marijuana laws. Citizens elsewhere may "prize their individuality and . . . control over their own lifestyles" as much as Alaskans, but few other courts are comparably sensitive to the right to privacy. For better or for worse, repeal of criminal penalties is mostly up to the state legislatures. In the next several years, they may rid us of the marijuana laws. If they do, it will not be because marijuana is hated and feared less. Almost no one really believes the old myths anymore. It will be because marijuana users are hated and feared less. They are becoming just like everybody else. A crime is in process of disappearing.

4
Drug Use:
How the Law Creates Crime

If possession of narcotics for personal use were no crime, if addicts were maintained on the drugs they require, related crimes of burglary and muggings would decline, and so would disease and death.

The Federal narcotics agents were on a dangerous assignment. An informer had led them to what they were told was a giant laboratory for the production of phencyclidine hydrochloride (PCP), a powerful hallucinogenic drug. It was on a forty-acre wooded site in the far northern part of California. The laboratory was guarded, so the story went, by two ferocious St. Bernard dogs.

Nineteen heavily armed men participated in the raid, some from the Federal Bureau of Narcotics and Dangerous Drugs and others from the Humboldt County sheriff's office. It was a simultaneous land and air attack, part of the raiding force arriving in a borrowed Army helicopter. Three reporters were taken along for the brave show.

The forty-acre site was occupied by Dirk Dickenson, twenty-four, and his girl friend, Judy Arnold. They were refugees from the city who had built a cabin in the woods and supported themselves by turning some of the trees on their property into furniture. When the helicopter first appeared overhead, they waved at the

51

occupants. But when it landed and armed men, none of them in police uniforms, burst from its door, Dickenson panicked and ran. A Federal narcotics agent shot him in the back and killed him. No drug laboratory was found.

Dirk Dickenson died on April 4, 1972. By then, the Bureau of Narcotics and Dangerous Drugs (BNDD) was acquiring a bad odor. Its agents had achieved a certain notoriety ripping up people's homes, sometimes because of mistaken tips from informers and other times because they got the addresses wrong. The agency was notorious for its corruption, its use of entrapment, and its ineffectuality in dealing with the main source of public concern about drugs: heroin.

The Bureau tried to acquire a new look. It even got a new name, the Drug Enforcement Agency. But three years later, in 1975, the DEA was in trouble. New scandals were reported, involving sex and bribery. The DEA's director resigned under fire. The General Accounting Office, a congressional agency established to monitor Federal executive agencies, reported that in fiscal 1974 the DEA had recovered only $160,000 of the $4 million it had spent to purchase drugs for use in evidence against drug dealers. The rest of the money had added to the monetary rewards of dealing. And, the perennial lament—the DEA was ineffectual in stemming the traffic in heroin.

Most of the criticisms of the BNDD and its successor, the DEA, were entirely justified. If anything, the agency deserved much harsher attack. In one major respect, however, the critics were unfair. The flow of heroin could not be significantly disrupted by the very best of law-enforcement agencies. What little police agencies can possibly do about narcotics—and it isn't much—virtually demands corrupt, abusive, and unethical practices.

Efforts to enforce laws against all "victimless" crimes require sleazy practices. No one steps forward to complain that someone sold him heroin, or marijuana, or traded sex for cash. To deal with these matters, police must pose as eager customers, tap telephones, or burst through doors unannounced. It must be very frustrating to try to enforce the drug laws. You get attacked either for the methods you use or for the inefficacy of your efforts.

It is harder by far to enforce the laws against possession of heroin than against any other victimless crime. That is because heroin has one unique characteristic: It is an extraordinarily addictive drug. Addicts will do almost anything to get it. Movies from *The Man with the Golden Arm* to *French Connection II* have exaggerated the horrors of withdrawal—or "cold turkey"—but simultaneously belittled the addictive strength of heroin. Once the movie's hero has suffered through withdrawal, they suggest, his addiction has been cured. In offering us this myth, these movies about the terrors of heroin addiction may have unintentionally contributed to the problem. The danger of using heroin seems smaller if the putative addict thinks dependence on the drug can be ended by a single horribly painful episode of withdrawal. It becomes almost a test of manliness to use heroin and, thereby, to declare readiness to take "cold turkey."

The enormous and varied efforts to discover "cures" for heroin addiction over the last century have resulted in an unbroken series of failures. If addicts are put in prison for long periods, go through withdrawal, and have no access to drugs while there, they are still addicted. When they get out, they return to opiates. If narcotics are gradually withdrawn in hospitals, when they get free, addicts return to opiates. If they receive psychological or psychiatric treatment, they return to opiates. If they enter therapeutic communities—many of them loudly touted for their successes—they relapse when they leave those communities, if not before. Treatment with other drugs does not "cure" addiction. The total failure of everything tried so far does not mean that the effort to find a cure should end. It does mean that social policy cannot be constructed on the false hope that a treatment has been discovered, or will shortly be available, to enable addicts to free themselves of dependence on opium derivatives.

There are, of course, a number of people who describe themselves as ex-addicts, sometimes with chiliastic fervor. A very few really have overcome their addictions. Others used heroin but never became addicted. Others are ex-addicts only until they relapse into addiction, and still others are simply misrepresenting themselves. Many missionaries, some from religious faiths and some from therapeutic communities, derive substantial income from their claim to cure addiction. There are always people willing to act a part for them.

The powerful and usually lasting addictive characteristics of the opium derivatives do not make them inherently devastating drugs. Another element is needed to bring about the havoc now caused by heroin: the laws purporting to limit its use.

In and of itself, heroin is not particularly dangerous or debilitating. People very rarely die of overdoses of heroin and certainly not from overdoses of the low grade of heroin commonly available in the streets. Soldiers in Vietnam ingested heroin of many times the strength of any commercially available in the United States and were not killed by it. It is generally estimated it would take a dose of about 500 milligrams of heroin to kill an unaddicted adult. Someone with an acquired tolerance for heroin could probably survive much larger doses. By contrast, a bag of heroin purchased on the streets of New York City might contain 10 milligrams. While there is some unevenness in the strength of heroin in a bag, the economies of the trade prevent addicts from ever getting anything remotely potent enough to kill them. The OD is a myth.

Addicts do die from injecting themselves with heroin, but not from overdoses. They die in great numbers from the diseases they get from dirty needles; from their own malnutrition, which comes from spending all the cash they can get on heroin; from the combined effects of other drugs they take along with heroin; and from the effects of the adulterants used to dilute heroin.

Heroin addiction can be treated, even if addicts cannot be freed from it. Addicts can obtain maintenance doses of drugs such as methadone. This drug has three major advantages over heroin. It is usually taken orally, which eliminates the danger of dirty needles. If taken orally, it does not produce the euphoria of heroin and therefore allows the addict to live a more steady existence.

And it need not be taken as often as heroin. Once a day, rather than two or three or four times a day, should suffice for even the most severely addicted.

About 75,000 persons are now enrolled in methadone-maintenance programs. While estimates vary enormously, a good guess is that this is about one-third of all heroin addicts in the United States. Those who have not enrolled in methadone-maintenance programs have many and varied reasons for not doing so. They include:

1. There is no program available to them. Three or four years ago, there were very long waiting periods to get into methadone programs. Today, most addicts who seek methadone maintenance can get it.

2. The bureaucratic or tyrannical character of some maintenance programs discourages addicts from enrolling.

3. Some addicts are as misinformed as other people about the possibility of a cure. They resist methadone maintenance.

4. Addicts still seek the euphoric "high" (or "rush" of relief from anxiety, as some experts regard it) of heroin and are not content with mere maintenance on a drug that relieves craving but does not give great pleasure.

5. None of the above. Some addicts just don't function very well and don't choose rational alternatives.

Of these reasons, the most important is number 4, the addict's insistence on heroin "highs." The Calvinist part of our heritage frowns on this. In devising public policies, our preference for methadone over heroin as a maintenance drug may have more to do with our stern disapproval of indulging the pleasure drive of addicts than with the very real practical advantages of methadone.

The public benefit of getting the great majority of addicts into maintenance programs would be enormous. It would drive down the price of illegal heroin and thereby drive most illegal purveyors out of business. Those who did purchase drugs illegally would get them at low enough prices so as not to have to engage in extensive property crime to pay for their habits. Addicts could live much more normal lives, holding jobs and maintaining their families. And most addicts could be freed from the dirty needles and the other concomitants of illegal heroin use that damage their health and kill so many of them.

I do not want to exaggerate the amount of property crime that could be eliminated. It was an overstatement by then Governor Nelson Rockefeller that addicts stealing to pay for drugs were responsible for half the property crime in New York.[1] And while addicts do cause a great deal of property crime, not nearly all of it could be eliminated if they no longer needed money to purchase drugs. Many addicts were shoplifting and burglarizing before they ever used heroin and would continue doing so even if relieved of the need to pay premium prices for drugs.

While I resist claiming too much, there would clearly be a noticeable decline in property crime if a great many more addicts were enrolled in maintenance programs. Some addicts are wholly consumed by their efforts to obtain drugs, and commit a great many crimes in pursuit of their goal. They might still commit crimes, but fewer. Other addicts are unable to function in jobs or families because of their illegal use of heroin. If they got maintenance doses of drugs at clinics, they could live much more normal lives and might abandon crime.

Elimination of the bureaucratic obstacles to the enrollment of addicts in methadone-maintenance programs is a matter of high priority. Perhaps even more important, and certainly a great deal more controversial, I believe we need a program of extensive experimentation with heroin maintenance. It was in widespread use in the United States in the World War I period and for a few years thereafter, apparently with considerable success. Many thousands of addicts were treated. Addiction was then at least as pervasive as it is today and was a severe medical problem. However, it was not a crime problem. Crime came only after revenue agents began enforcing regulations promulgated in January 1915 by the Department of the Treasury after adoption of the Harrison Act. They closed down the maintenance clinics by about 1923.[2]

The best-known, though perhaps least understood, use of heroin maintenance is in England. While I believe we should borrow from the British experience in trying to solve the addiction problem in the United States, some enormous differences in the problem must be enumerated:

1. There are perhaps a hundred times as many heroin addicts in the United States as in Britain.

2. Heroin addiction is not perceived as a race problem in Britain. It is not disproportionately an affliction of immigrants from the Indian subcontinent, Africa, or the West Indies.

3. Heroin is not encumbered by the mythology in Britain that surrounds it in the United States. A doctor may prescribe it as a treatment for a child with a bad cough. Anything of that sort would produce violent outrage in the United States.

4. Doctors in Britain do not think it is immoral to treat addicts with heroin. A Calvinist antagonism to its perceived pleasure giving is not a part of the problem in the British approach to addiction.

5. There is not a giant cure-and-enforcement industry in Britain. By contrast, there may be as many or more people professionally employed to fight narcotics in the United States as there are addicts in this country. We spend billions of dollars trying to cure or punish addicts. The people paid with this money have careers built on antagonism to any possible use of heroin.

6. There is not a large industry in Britain living off the illegal sale of heroin. One reason is that it is so much more profitable to sell heroin to Americans. England has never been a very attractive market for the international drug trade because it never created a black market price through absolute prohibition.[3]

Despite all these differences, I believe the current British approach should be emulated, at least experimentally, in the United States. Doctors practicing in clinics should be free to treat addicts by administering heroin. As in England, the addict would not have the right to demand heroin. Its availability would depend on a doctor's decision that the administration of heroin is the right method of treatment.

I do not favor allowing doctors to write prescriptions for

heroin addicts. Such a system, abandoned in England in 1968, had been blamed for an upsurge in the number of addicts. The increase in addiction was minuscule by American standards, but very worrisome to the British. Their expressions of concern led Americans to believe that the rise in addiction demonstrated the failure of the British system. The British, on the other hand, saw it as a reason to tighten control over their system by centralizing it in clinics and barring individual practitioners from prescribing heroin. The vast size of the heroin trade in the United States makes it essential that any heroin-maintenance program here model itself on the present British system rather than on the pre-1968 version.

Opponents of heroin maintenance in the United States have a cluster of objections [journalist Horace Judson notes] often put with great emotional intensity—against the characteristics of the drug itself: that addicts given the choice will always prefer heroin, that it is not possible to stabilize heroin dosages, that heroin addicts lead chaotic lives. To these assertions, the English experience I think makes a clear response: heroin addicts differ; there can be stable heroin addicts, able to manage their doses and their lives, though these may not be the most usual and certainly are not the most noticeable; a clinic that offers sensible psychiatric and social services besides drugs, and where the physician can select other drugs besides heroin, can help a high proportion of its clients to live more healthily, more sanely, more effectively in society.[4]

The most important objection to heroin-maintenance clinics in the United States is that people would be encouraged to use the drug in the first instance because if they became addicted they could get it free at clinics. The tiny number of addicts in England—perhaps 2,500—hardly suggests anyone has been led to heroin addiction because they would later get it free. On the contrary, I believe this is one important reason there are so few addicts in England.

Sale or distribution of heroin for other than medical purposes is a crime in England as in the United States. But although the laws in the United States carry more severe penalties than in England, the laws are violated here with far greater frequency. The price that can be obtained for the illegal sale of heroin in England provides little incentive to risk the penalties. For most of the past century, illegal heroin has sold in the United States at between ten and twenty times the price it commanded in England.

As long as the economic incentives exist, the illegal sale of heroin cannot be stopped. Opium poppies can grow in most countries of the world and in many parts of the United States. A few square miles can produce enough poppies to supply the entire American addict population. If no poppies are grown, synthetic versions of the drug can be readily manufactured. Heroin is the most compact of contrabands. Searching out the tiny amounts needed to supply American addicts from the luggage and persons of hundreds of millions of travelers crossing American borders each year and from the vast quantities of goods shipped here is like trying to find a needle in a whole field full of haystacks. With luck and informers, some part of the illegal heroin supply can be stopped. Even then, the informers often tip off customs agents or police because they resent business rivals undercutting their prices. Our law-enforcement effort is manipulated to serve price-fixing purposes. If the price is right, the heroin usually gets through.

One way to force a drastic reduction in the price of heroin in the United States would be to stop prosecuting its purveyors. That remedy probably would produce a great increase in the number of people using heroin. The only alternative method of cutting the cost of heroin I can imagine is to make it available free to addicts in clinics. It is the way England has chosen, and it has made it uneconomic to dispense heroin illegally.

The immense differences between England and the United States prevent me from now proposing an all-out program of heroin maintenance. Experimentation seems the more prudent course. Experiments should be designed to determine the impact of heroin-maintenance programs on the distribution of illegal heroin and on the number of new recruits to the addict population. They should start, therefore, in cities with relatively small addict populations far removed from major centers of narcotics distribution. Minneapolis, Honolulu, and Portland come to mind as good places to begin. The impact on those cities could be readily measured. An experimental program in New York City could hardly have much impact. But if the illegal sale of heroin could be drastically reduced in a city such as Minneapolis by its administration free of charge to addicts in medical clinics, a program of heroin maintenance might be justified in New York.

My proposal envisions the removal of all criminal penalties from persons possessing small quantities of narcotics for their own use. Sale and distribution would remain major crimes. The point is to try to diminish the rewards while maintaining severe penalties for selling heroin.

Cocaine, barbiturates, and amphetamines are both less dangerous and more dangerous than heroin. They are less dangerous in the sense that they are not comparably addictive. They are much more dangerous in the sense that the physical damage they do is enormous. Heroin's physical damages are attributable to dirty needles, adulterants, the circumstances in which the drug is taken, and the laws penalizing addiction. Cocaine, amphetamines, and barbiturates do the damage themselves.

The damage done by heroin is largely a creation of public policy. Changing public policy is an important way of undoing that damage. Public policy is less centrally relevant to some other drugs. Only small steps can be taken to reform public policy to mitigate the damage.

The first and most useful reform of public policy would be to stop making possession of any drug for a person's own use a crime. The prohibition approach to drugs—alcohol, heroin, cocaine, or whatever—is a demonstrated failure. It criminalizes a lot of people without preventing the use of the drugs.

Second, the focus of public policy should shift from trying to stamp out these drugs—a present impossibility because of the price they command where they are illicit and the ease with which they can be produced and transported—to trying to mitigate the damage they do. This is the principal thrust of a series of recommendations by the Consumers Union,[5] and it makes a great deal of sense. A law making it a crime to possess hypodermic needles for injection of heroin, the Consumers Union notes, "leads to the use of nonsterile needles, to the sharing of needles, and to epidemics of hepatitis and other crippling, sometimes fatal, needle-borne diseases."[6] Similarly, drug users should be warned, the Consumers Union suggests, that some drugs "should be taken orally if at all; the *injection* of amphetamines or cocaine in large doses constitutes one of the most damaging forms of drug use known to man."[7]

The "war on drugs" has led nowhere. If drugs had been stamped out by such methods as used by the Drug Enforcement Agency and its predecessors, the war might be justified. In practice, the "war on drugs" has been a war on drug users and on such chance victims as Dirk Dickenson in his cabin in the woods of northern California. Drugs have flourished and so has the criminal network that feeds on their very illegality. The laws on drugs thus create and promote crime. They involve the police and the courts and the prisons in wasted time and wasted money.

5

Take Away All Guns

June 1971. The publication of excerpts from "The Pentagon Papers" by *The New York Times* and *The Washington Post* had precipitated a fast and furious legal battle. An appellate court in Washington, D.C., had just ruled in favor of the *Post* but had stayed its own decision to give the government time to appeal. To get the stay lifted, and continue publication the next day, the *Post*'s attorneys would have to go to the Chief Justice of the United States, the Honorable Warren E. Burger. The newspaper's attorneys were at work on their legal papers and were expected at Burger's home sometime that evening. Several reporters camped nearby to observe the scene.

As the evening wore on, a couple of the reporters decided to ring Burger's front door bell to let him know they were there. The Chief Justice of the United States answered the door, a six-shooter in his hand.

A great many Americans have guns at home to protect themselves. A gun, they believe, guards them against would-be robbers, burglars, or rapists. It is used many times more often to shoot themselves, their husbands or wives, their children, their parents, their neighbors, or anybody else with whom they might have a spat. When it is fired at another person, more likely than not, the shooter is drunk at the time. At a three-foot range, even a drunk can put a hole in a vital organ.

Some of the damage done by guns is accidental. In the little village where I rented a cottage for weekends, sixteen-year-old David was demonstrating the loading and unloading of his new 12-gauge shotgun to his fifteen-year-old friend and high school classmate Nadia. He discharged it into her right arm. Her arm had to be amputated. David was arrested and charged with second-degree assault. Both of them will be maimed for life—he by his arrest record, she by the loss of her right arm.

David N. Gary walked into a second-grade parochial school classroom in Penns Grove, New Jersey, and shot and wounded the teacher. When the principal arrived to see what was happening, Gary shot him dead. Curtis Poindexter did his shooting in a courthouse, killing a judge and wounding the sheriff and deputy sheriff. No motive could be readily established for either shooting

David Gary and Curtis Poindexter are bush leaguers compared to the likes of a Charles Whitman or a Mark Essex. Whitman managed to kill fourteen people from his perch on the tower of the University of Texas before he, in turn, was gunned down. Essex did his shooting from the roof of the Howard Johnson motel in New Orleans and disposed of seven people before a bullet ended his life.

Of nearly 20,000 murders in the United States each year, two out of every three are committed with guns. Since murders are usually spur-of-the-moment products of arguments among friends, lovers, and relatives, most could be avoided if no guns were ready at hand. The same is also true of many serious assaults.

In 1973, the most recent year for which data are available, 53 percent of all murders were committed with handguns, 6 percent with rifles, and 8 percent with shotguns. In 1973, there were 416,270 aggravated assaults reported to the FBI by local law-enforcement agencies. Aggravated assault is defined by the Bureau as "an unlawful attack by one person upon another for the purpose of inflicting severe bodily injury usually accompanied by the use of a weapon or other means likely to produce death or serious bodily harm. Attempts are included." If guns figured more often in aggravated assaults, more aggravated assaults would turn into murders. Still, aggravated assaults with guns accounted for 25.7 percent of the total, or upward of 100,000.

The FBI figures also disclose that 160,000 robberies were committed with guns in 1973, out of a total of about 250,000 armed robberies and out of the approximate total of 380,000 robberies and muggings. Adding a certain number of rapes committed by criminals armed with guns, about 300,000 gun crimes are included among the fewer than 900,000 serious crimes of violence reported to the FBI in a year by local police departments. Because they involve guns, they are the violent crimes that do the most damage. Besides, thousands of Americans kill themselves with guns each year, and tens of thousands accidentally injure themselves and others.

No one knows how many guns are privately owned by American citizens. The FBI says there are 90 million—24 million handguns, 35 million rifles, and 31 million shotguns. Most other estimates run higher. Some guesses run as high as 200 million. The number of handguns is often put at between 40 and 45 million.

The problem seems beyond remedy. Certainly it would not do much good to ban the manufacture or import of "Saturday night specials," the cheap guns that have acted as a lightning rod for much criticism of the American gun mania. "The upshot of it all will be," journalist Robert Sherrill has pointed out, "that the manufacturers of cheap guns will be driven out of business and replaced by the manufacturers of less-than-cheap guns, but the outpouring of small weapons onto the American market will not change in the slightest. It will only have the U.S. seal of approval. The established old-line gun industry will see that as a great victory." [1] Reducing the number of purveyors of handguns or requiring waiting periods before guns can be purchased, both proposals favored by President Gerald Ford, would have no great effect. Even eliminating all gun sales would not have a very large effect. There are far too many guns already in circulation.

Registration of guns and gun owners is generally perceived as a more severe restriction than those proposed by President Ford.

The National Rifle Association (NRA), an extraordinarily well organized lobbying group and the principal spokesman for the nation's gun enthusiasts, is violently opposed to registration. On the other hand, the NRA is "heartened" by President Ford's proposals.

Gerald Ford's Attorney General, Edward Levi, would have gone beyond registration. He would have prohibited handgun ownership in high-crime areas. Levi's proposal sounds like a way of saying blacks should not be allowed to have handguns while whites should be able to keep their guns. Put that way, this is an idea many individual members of the NRA would probably welcome. Nevertheless, the NRA and the rest of the gun lobby reacted apoplectically to the Attorney General's suggestion, perhaps because they understood that, by comparison with countries in which gun ownership is not prevalent, the entire United States is a high-crime area.

I favor outright prohibition of all private ownership of guns. All guns. This proposition seems to me as sensible as prohibiting private ownership of nuclear weapons. In each of the thirty years since the United States devastated Nagasaki with an atomic bomb, Americans have committed comparable mayhem on themselves and each other with guns.

Gun owners will, of course, assert that prohibition would deprive them of a fundamental right guaranteed by the Constitution, "the right to bear arms." I do not believe the Constitution guarantees any such "right." It is only when the words are lifted out of context that they appear to secure an unqualified right to own guns. As historian Irving Brant points out,

The Second Amendment, popularly misread, comes to life chiefly on the parade floats of rifle associations and the propaganda of mail-order houses selling pistols to teen-age gangsters: "A well regulated Militia, being necessary to the security of a free State, the right of the people to keep and bear Arms, shall not be infringed." As the wording reveals, this article relates entirely to the militia—a fact that was made even clearer by a clause dropped from Madison's original wording: "but no person religiously scrupulous of bearing arms should be compelled to render military service in person." It was made clearest of all in the congressional debate on the amendment. Why was a militia necessary to "the security of a free state"? Elbridge Gerry asked and answered that question: "What, sir, is the use of the militia? It is to prevent the establishment of a standing army, the bane of liberty." Thus the purpose of the Second Amendment was to forbid Congress to prohibit the maintenance of a state militia. By its nature, that amendment cannot be transformed into a personal right to bear arms, enforceable by federal compulsion upon the state.[2]

To Brant's historical analysis I would add that, to my knowledge, none of the organizations lobbying for the right to bear arms is also seeking to disband our gigantic standing army, "the bane of liberty." On the contrary, the same people who seek absolute protection for private ownership of guns seem to be among the most vigorous supporters of a national military policy that runs exactly counter to the philosophy of the Second Amendment.

Aside from their dubious constitutional claims, gun owners have many arguments for keeping their weapons. Millions of Americans are hunters, and they vigorously contest any threats to their sport. For myself, I confess never to have found much charm in slaughter. If hunters insist upon a reason to stalk our remaining forests, perhaps they should be allowed one. They should be made to revert to bows and arrows. These weapons would be much more cumbersome for holdup men than shotguns and wouldn't do for an assassin or a crazed Charles Whitman nearly as well as rifles. But the bow and arrow ought to be very attractive to hunters. It would give the animals in the forest a much better sporting chance and could be at least as much a symbol of manliness as the long guns hunters now cherish.

Target shooters also insist on their right to indulge in hitting bull's-eyes. Let them throw darts. In Britain, where dart throwing is popular, few people accidentally kill or maim themselves or each other while cleaning darts. But dart throwing is as great a test of skill as target shooting and seems to lend itself much more nicely to merriment and bonhomie. The clinching argument, I suggest, is that dart throwers could practice in any corner tavern. Target shooters in the United States also practice in taverns occasionally, and thereby increase the mortality rates of bartenders and patrons. Generally, however, target shooters are confined to inconvenient shooting ranges.

Gun owners also like to think of themselves as armed citizens protecting their homes and their property. "It is a phantasmagoria of roscoes," says Sherrill. "It is a panorama of holdupmen beaten to the draw by crafty shopkeepers and of highwaymen come riding, riding, riding up to the old inn door, only to be met by a timely half ounce of lead." [3] To the proposition that they will have less to fear from holdup men and highwaymen if guns are prohibited to all, they respond with a slogan: "When guns are outlawed, only outlaws will have guns."

There are no reported statistics on the number of criminals apprehended or shot dead by "armed citizens." Whenever something of the sort happens, the diligent scouts from the National Rifle Association ferret out the details and publish them. But, without challenging the NRA reports, it should also be noted that the number of "armed citizens" who mistakenly shoot themselves, their families, and innocent passersby far exceeds their actual bag of criminals. As for the general proposition that guns should remain legal to permit citizens to engage in self-defense, it seems analogous to arguing that smallpox should be encouraged so that people may build up antibodies. The disease may kill us all.

A political variant on the "armed citizen" sees him resisting a domestic tyrant or a foreign invader. In this chimerical vision, American gun owners could wage such effective guerrilla warfare as to ensure that, as the slogan on New Hampshire's automobile license plates puts it, they would "live free or die." When it comes to domestic tyrants, the ones I can imagine would find most gun owners their willing accomplices. As for foreign invasion, assuming there are survivors of the nuclear holocaust that would precede it, there ought to be time for the government to issue weapons to would-be guerrillas. The Vietcong demonstrated that people didn't have to be lifelong gun owners to wage effective guerrilla warfare.

During each year of the Vietnam war, gun owners killed and maimed more Americans in the streets back home than fell as victims in the jungles of Southeast Asia. Guerrilla warfare in the streets is not just a fantasy to be lived out when an invader strikes. Without benefit of any invasion, it takes place all the time on the sidewalks, in homes, and in taverns. The frontier may have long since disappeared, but half the homeowners on the block still fancy themselves as Daniel Boone or Kit Carson. For want of marauding grizzly bears to shoot, they turn their weapons on their wives, husbands, and neighbors. They have made each other the targets in a national shooting gallery.

The difficulty with my proposal to ban all guns, of course, is that gun ownership is so widespread as to make prohibitions impossible to enforce. Impossible, that is, without the draconian measures I oppose. Another armed nation's recent effort to take guns from its citizens is instructive.

In March 1975, Jamaica adopted new gun-control legislation. It gave citizens two weeks to turn in unlicensed guns. Thereafter, the police, reinforced for this effort by the army, would engage in systematic searches and seizures. No warrants were required. Anyone found with an unlicensed gun after the grace period could be imprisoned for life.

A lot of guns were turned in during the two weeks after the new law went into effect. But Jamaican authorities believed many people illegally kept their guns. Some Jamaicans woke up one morning to find an entire section of Kingston surrounded by soldiers with bayonets while other soldiers conducted house-to-house searches for guns. People were arbitrarily stopped and searched on the streets and in their cars. Anyone found with a gun or ammunition was immediately jailed. There was no provision for release pending trial in specially established gun courts.

The gun laws in Jamaica also provided for the censorship of movies and television programs to eliminate all scenes showing gunplay. "If you regard yourself as seriously at war with crime," Jamaica's Prime Minister Michael Manley told an American television interviewer, "that is the sort of power that you have to have, or you're joking if you don't have that power. And we regard ourselves as being at war with crime. One man may—may be found in illegal possession of a firearm who, in fact, is one of the people who is trying to shoot society to pieces."

The powers exercised by the Jamaican government in enforcing the gun laws led the country's leading civil liberties lawyer, Ian Ramsey, to say, "I think that we're witnessing, on what is supposed to be a legal basis, the probable beginning of a dictatorship." As urgent as the need is to get rid of guns, that is far too stiff a price to pay.

The alternative is to adopt legislation prohibiting the import, manufacture, sale, and possession of guns and ammunition in full knowledge that, at least insofar as possession is concerned, the law is unenforceable. While this is an unhappy prospect, the other choices seem worse still. At least these prohibitions could effectively prevent still more weapons from getting into the hands of Americans. With the enormous number now around, the impact would be small. Prohibiting sales of ammunition would be slightly more effective, though undoubtedly many gun owners would stock up during the long periods of debate that would precede legislation. In a grace period for turning in guns after the adoption of legislation, fair value should be paid for weapons turned in. This would provide some extra incentive to turn in guns, though it would be rash to hold out great hopes.

The worst consequence of such legislation would be the likely creation of an enormous underground market for the illegal sale of weapons. It could come to resemble the trade in alcohol during Prohibition or the present trade in illegal drugs. The possibility that this could happen is sufficient to make any advocate of gun control despair.

While the principled differences between handguns and long guns are not apparent, it is easy to understand the reasoning of those who would restrict prohibitions to easily concealed weapons. They hope to avoid the adamant opposition of all the rifle and shotgun owners as well as of the people who possess handguns. But rifles are used in political assassinations as often as handguns. Sawed-off shotguns get used in a lot of robberies. Both kinds of long guns are used with some frequency to punctuate arguments in a deadly way. If handguns weren't available, long guns would be used even more often. Rap Brown once said, "Violence is as American as cherry pie." In committing violence, you use whatever weapon comes to hand. Adoption and enforcement of antigun legislation are so difficult, however, it is hard to fault a strategy limited to banning handguns. I endorse such prohibitions, but only as a step in the right direction.

Some guns are in the hands of the criminal population. Most guns belong to usually law-abiding people. In speculating on the prospect of disobedience to antigun legislation, I do not differentiate between these two groups. If anything, I suspect that the "law-abiding" people would be more disobedient. They are better off and therefore would be less tempted by cash reimbursements for turning in guns. The disregard hunters demonstrate for posted private property is a clue to their priorities. More important, "law-abiding" gun owners would see defiance of antigun laws as a matter of principle. If gun owners didn't believe their own rhetoric, it might be possible to stop Americans from pumping bullets into each other. But they do believe it. The worst thing about the National Rifle Association and its supporters is that they are sincere.

"I am one who believes that law-abiding, responsible citizens have a constitutional right to own weapons—whether for protection of home and family or for legitimate sport," the Honorable Robert L. F. Sikes told his colleagues in the House of Representatives at a hearing in February 1975. Sikes, a Floridian and one of the most powerful members of the House, served on the National Board of the National Rifle Association for some of the many years he has spent in Congress. His stance as a spokesman for the interests of the "law-abiding" has not hindered him from growing very rich through business deals made possible by his exercise of public power, according to a series of articles in *The New York Times*. "The enemy we seek to control is not firearms," according to Sikes, "it is crime and criminals. Extreme anti-gun proposals could simply take guns away from those who are victims of crime, not the criminals." That is what "law-abiding" gun owners believe. Because they believe it, there is little chance they would abide by antigun laws.

Elsewhere in this book, I propose that the state do less. Here, I want the state to do more. I want the state to take away people's guns. But I don't want the state to use methods against gun owners that I deplore when used in enforcement of laws against naughty children, sexual minorities, drug users, and unsightly drinkers. Since such reprehensible police practices are probably needed to make antigun laws effective, my proposal to ban all guns should probably be marked a failure before it is even tried.

6

Police Crime:
The Rotten Barrel

"Hey—where's the graft money?" yelled the voice on the other side of the door. The plant manager excused himself for a moment, took an envelope from his desk, and handed it to the uniformed policeman who stood there waiting for it as the door opened. That piece of business completed, the meeting continued.

This scene took place in 1956. I was a college student employed for the summer as a labor union intern. It was a Sunday afternoon at a small manufacturing firm in a residential section of Brooklyn. Negotiations were under way in an effort to head off a strike. As always when business was good, the plant was operating on Sunday in violation of an antinoise ordinance. The policeman had been by to collect the regular payoff to the local precinct for ignoring the violation.

As a not very worldly-wise nineteen-year-old, I was startled by the incident. It wasn't the corruption. I wasn't *that* naïve. My amazement was at the unabashed shout for "graft money." I had thought such things were done more subtly.

They usually are done a bit more subtly. In the two decades since that incident in Brooklyn, I have never again heard a policeman ask for "graft money" in so many words. But, like every big-city resident, I have seen my share of corruption. A lot of it is minor—police leaving luncheonettes without bothering to pay for their meals, or merchants double-parking cars and trucks near

72

their businesses with complete assurance they will not be ticketed. Some of it—such as a policeman arresting somebody to settle a private grudge for a store owner for whom the officer moonlighted as a guard—is more serious.

Police corruption in New York City is different from corruption in other cities in one major respect: It is better documented. The Knapp Commission investigation in the early 1970s, the Seabury investigation in the early 1930s, and the Lexow Committee investigation of 1894 demonstrate its persistence. All the investigators agreed on one conclusion: It isn't a problem of a "few rotten apples in the barrel," as police defenders often put it. The barrel is rotten. "Of course, not all policemen are corrupt," the Knapp Commission conceded in its August 1972 final report. "If we are to exclude such paltry infractions as free meals, an appreciable number do not engage in any corrupt activities. Yet, with extremely rare exceptions, even those who themselves engage in no corrupt activities are involved in corruption in the sense that they take no steps to prevent what they know or suspect to be going on about them."

Chicago is the second city, not only in size but in the documentation of the corruption of its police force. In 1928, a special grand jury said the Chicago Police Department was "rotten to the core," a charge echoed by the 1931 report of the Federal government's Wickersham Commission. In 1960, the department was rocked by a scandal unusual even in the sorry history of police crime. A burglar revealed that he had been hired to steal merchandise by Chicago police officers while they cruised the neighborhood as lookouts. That incident was a factor in persuading Mayor Richard Daley to bring in a professor of criminology, O. W. Wilson, as police commissioner. Daley needed a commissioner without any taint of previous connection with the Chicago police. But while Wilson himself was honest, as a lone outsider in charge of a large department, he was limited in the reforms he could institute. In 1973, nineteen police officers were convicted for a series of tavern shakedowns reaching back into the Wilson years.

The incidence of police corruption in Chicago and other

cities was demonstrated by a remarkable study undertaken by Albert J. Reiss, Jr., on behalf of the President's Commission on Law Enforcement. In the summer of 1966, thirty-six observers spent eight-hour tours of duty riding with police on patrol over a period of about seven weeks. The cities selected for the study were Boston, Chicago, and Washington, D.C. "Counting all felonies and misdemeanors, except assaults on citizens," Reiss reports on the basis of the information submitted by the observers, "roughly 1 in 5 officers were observed in criminal violation of the law. There was some variation among the three cities in the crime patterns of police officers and the rate of violation." This was true, the observers found, even though "The types of opportunities and situations that give rise to officers violating criminal statutes are relatively few. Opportunities arise principally in relationship with businesses and businessmen, policing traffic violators and deviants, and controlling evidence from crime. Obtaining money or merchandise illegally is the principal officer violation." In tabulating "criminal" violations, Reiss's observers did not include much of what is properly regarded as police corruption. Putting this into a separate category, Reiss writes:

A gray area of offending also exists. Many businessmen in a community engage in exchanges or practices with police officers that from the standpoint of the law could bring charges of bribery. A variety of such practices were uncovered in our observations of the police including almost daily free meals, drinks, or cigarettes, the profferment of gifts marking anniversaries and holidays, and discounts on purchases. Such practices are specifically prohibited by the rules and regulations of any police department and subject to disciplinary action if "officially" discovered. Within each of the cities, one-third (31 percent) of all businessmen in wholesale or retail trade or business and repair services in the high-crime-rate areas openly acknowledged favors to policemen. Of those giving favors, 43 percent said they gave free merchandise, food or services to all policemen; the remainder did so at discount. When observers were present with officers during their eight-hour tour of duty, for almost one of every three of the 841 tours (31 percent), the officers did not pay for their meals. For the remaining cases, small discounts were common.[1]

The extraordinary thing is that police officers engaged in all this corruption in full awareness that observers for a presidential commission were watching all their actions. It seems likely that there would have been even more criminal behavior by the police if the observers had not been present. Criminal behavior in the presence of the observers should have been deterred by fear that pledges of confidentiality might be broken, by the naturally inhibiting presence of an outsider, and by awareness that the criminal behavior would turn up in statistical reports besmirching their calling. The willingness of police to exhibit criminal behavior to observers suggests it is so ingrained they cannot readily act any differently.

Police corruption is most visible in big-city ghettos. So, too, are all the other vices of the police profession: discourtesy to citizens; unresponsiveness to complaints of crime; "cooping," or sleeping on the job; unequal enforcement of the law; entrapment; unreasonable searches; lying; and brutality. The police precinct in a black neighborhood often has the look of a military fortress uneasily occupying a hostile nation. Not the place a victim of crime would want to go to report an injury or a loss. Even less the place a witness to crime who would derive no personal profit from the effort would go to tell what he knows.

As police are among the first to concede, there is a great deal more crime than is ever reported to them. There is several times as much larceny as is ever reported to the police. Burglary, assault, and rape are also greatly underreported. Even armed robbery is often not reported. According to various studies, the actual incidence of property crime and violent crime may range from almost twice as much to five times as much as is reported. The principal variable in determining how much crime is actually reported appears to be a community's attitude toward the police.

Within cities, the greatest underreporting of crime is from ghetto communities. In part, this is because the victims can rarely get reimbursement for their losses from insurance companies, and they have no incentive to itemize their losses on tax returns. Verification of losses for these purposes is a powerful stimulus to the reporting of crime to police among well-to-do people. Dislike and distrust of the police greatly exacerbate underreporting by racial minorities. Yet these are precisely the people who are most severely victimized by crime. The disproportionate degree of their suffering can be judged from the incidence of the one universally reported crime: murder. In proportion to their numbers, blacks are murdered ten times as frequently as whites!

If police are to be of great value in controlling crime, they must get cooperation from citizens. They must be told about crimes. Witnesses must be willing to testify against criminals. And citizens must sense that they live in a law-abiding society. "Crime is contagious," as Justice Louis Brandeis put it. "If the government becomes a lawbreaker, it breeds contempt for law." Lawbreaking by the government, as most visibly symbolized by the police, has certainly bred contempt for law in many American ghetto communities. Police are not the cause of the crime problem in such communities. But the low esteem for the people charged with enforcing the law has certainly aggravated the problem.

In the early 1960s, a British royal commission issued a statement on the fine relations between the citizens and the police. "It is attested," said the commission, "by the foreign visitor whose favorable comments on our police are well known, and it is demonstrated in the common every-day instances in which people instinctively consult a policeman when in difficulty or perplexity even of a minor kind. . . . [T]here is a kind of relationship between the policeman and the man in the street in this country which is of the greatest value." To some Britons, the royal commission's statement seemed far too smug and self-satisfied. Certainly, the British police have their faults, and critics point them out. But massive police corruption is virtually inconceivable in Britain. By comparison with the United States, the royal commission's statement was entirely justified. The benefit to law enforcement in Britain is enormous. Crimes are almost invariably reported to the police, and the British police can count on public assistance in the performance of their duties.

A complete program to enhance respect for the police, which includes making the police worthy of respect, is beyond the scope of this book. Nevertheless, I offer a few proposals. They would, I think, effect a radical transformation in our police forces and in the cooperation they would get from citizens.

At present, entry into police forces takes place at either of two levels: at the very bottom or the very top. Nothing in between. Unless a person enters a force as commissioner of police or a deputy commissioner, the universal requirement of police departments across the country is that a new member of the force start at the very bottom. Promotion to command levels takes place only from within a particular police department. Not only is it impossible to enter a police department in the way a graduate of West Point or Annapolis enters the armed services; it is virtually unheard of for a person who has reached a command level in one department to move to a similar position in another department.

In its rigid requirement that people work their way up from within, police work is almost unique. (Municipal fire and sanitation departments follow similar practices.) This requirement has two very damaging consequences. First, it makes it extremely difficult to upgrade recruitment for police departments. Second, a person reaches a command level only by going along with the behavior patterns characteristic of a department. If that behavior includes corruption or brutality, the candidate for promotion must go along with it.

As the Knapp Commission noted, there is a "code of silence" in police departments. It makes tattling on a fellow officer the most heinous of sins. "Any policeman violating the code did so at his peril. The result," said the commission, is that the "rookie who comes into the Department is faced with the situation where it is easier to become corrupt than to remain honest." Albert Reiss's conclusion was similar: "The fact that mobility within police departments occurs almost exclusively by promotion from *within* a department makes line and staff officers subject to subversion by the line. They readily overlook practices and violations that are common among patrolmen either because they, themselves, engaged in them when they served as patrolmen or many of their friends did so." [2]

To deal with the problem of recruitment, the President's Commission on Law Enforcement proposed that departments in large and medium-size cities establish three classes of officers.[3] An elite group would be known as police agents. It would investigate major crimes, make difficult arrests, patrol high-crime and high-tension areas, enforce vice, gambling, and narcotics laws, and investigate crimes where juveniles are involved. A middle group would be known as police officers. It would perform routine patrol functions and enforce traffic laws. The final group would be known as community service officers. These would be young men between the ages of seventeen and twenty-one, largely recruited from minority groups, who would assist police agents and police officers in their work and who would improve communication with neighborhoods.

These proposals would have some value in disrupting the rigidity of police departments. To that extent, they would be welcome changes. But because they reflect an inadequate understanding of the nature of police work, and because they would still require socialization within a department before achieving command, I prefer to make alternative proposals.

What the President's Commission on Law Enforcement somewhat disparagingly described as "routine patrol" is the most important part of police work. As James Q. Wilson has noted, in police departments,

discretion increases as one moves *down* the hierarchy. . . . The patrolman is almost solely in charge of enforcing those laws that are the least precise, most ambiguous (those dealing with disorderly conduct, for example), or whose application is most sensitive to the availability of scarce resources and the policies of the administrator (those governing traffic offenses, for example). Detectives, by contrast, are concerned with the more precisely defined crimes ... and only after the crime has been committed. The patrolman handles matters about which there are apt to be great differences of public opinion; the detectives, except those dealing with vice and narcotics, deal with crimes whose definition and seriousness are not, typically, in dispute. Further, the patrolman is supposed not only to enforce laws but to maintain order and keep the peace; detectives are concerned almost entirely with law enforcement and hardly at all with peace keeping. Finally, patrolmen when not responding to a particular call are supposed to "prevent" crime, look for "suspicious" activities, and make "on view" arrests of persons breaking a law even though no one has summoned the police.[4]

In the years since the report of the President's Commission on Law Enforcement and the publication of Wilson's book, the relative importance of patrol has greatly increased. Police on patrol continue to exercise the vast discretion described by Wilson. The advent of the National Crime Information Center (NCIC) has added an important new element to police work.

Detective work, on the other hand, is of declining significance in the apprehension of persons suspected of committing major crimes. A May 11, 1975, story in *The New York Times* disclosed that a burglary squad detective in Manhattan will not investigate a case unless the loss is $10,000 or more. Elsewhere in New York City, a $5,000 loss is the cutoff point. These minimum requirements are so high that only very well-to-do persons can expect any kind of investigation to take place if their homes should be burglarized. It could easily lead to the mistaken assumption that burglars don't get caught, and, therefore, that crime pays. Nothing could be farther from the truth.

Burglars get caught, though not necessarily for any particular burglary. To make a career of burglary, they must repeat the crime very often. Sooner or later they get caught in the act. Probably sooner.

The FBI estimates that 2,540,900 burglaries occurred during 1973. These estimates include reported and unreported crimes in communities furnishing reports to the FBI. The Bureau also says the victims of these crimes suffered an aggregate loss of $856 million. That works out to about $337 a burglary. Some of that loss is in vandalism by the burglars. Very little of it is in cash. Since burglars must sell the appliances and furnishings they steal at far below their real value, it would be very surprising if they could net more than an average of $100 per burglary, even though their crimes cost the victims much more. An average full-time burglar trying to net $10,000 a year would have to commit 100 burglaries a year, or two a week.

The FBI also estimates that there were 434,000 burglary arrests in 1973. Using these statistics, one burglary in six resulted in arrest.[5] Our average full-time burglar would get caught within the first three weeks. On any cost-benefit analysis, burglary does not pay.

The enormous disparity between the loss in an average burglary and the loss necessary to trigger a police investigation demonstrates the tremendous dependence of police on patrol in apprehending criminals. Patrolling police may surprise a burglar in the act or respond to an alarm, complaint, or outcry. Five times out of six, the burglar may get away without arrest. But number six comes so quickly that the happenstance of arrest by patrol must be considered an extremely efficient way of dealing with such crimes.

The New York City Police Department's high cutoff point for investigating burglaries makes a great deal of sense. The burglars who commit those crimes need only commit them infrequently. Thereby, they diminish their exposure to a chance arrest to the point where investigation may be the efficient way of trying to apprehend them. Moreover, such crimes are easier to investigate. A loss of such size is more likely to involve identifiable paintings, jewelry, or other items that could be traced to a burglar.

Robbery, which involves the use or threatened use of force, is a far more serious crime than burglary. The average robbery costs its victims less than burglary—$261. However, since the loss is often cash, it is probably more profitable to the criminals. A full-time robber trying to net $10,000 a year would probably need to commit only about 50 such crimes a year, or one a week. Again, using the FBI's estimates, 382,680 robberies were committed in 1973, and 127,530 arrests were made. Since there are sometimes two or more persons arrested for a single robbery, the FBI estimates that 27 percent of all such crimes lead to arrest. Our hypothetical robber could expect to average less than four weeks before getting arrested.

Investigation is a tiny bit more of a factor in producing robbery arrests than arrests for burglaries. The victim often gets to see the criminal and can occasionally identify him from a mug shot. Immediate outcry to a passing patrolman is more likely in the case of robbery. Also, victims sometimes see robbers on a subsequent occasion, alert a passing patrolman, and secure an arrest.

Even assuming that there are three times as many burglaries as are estimated by the FBI and twice as many robberies—reasonable guesses—a full-time burglar earning $10,000 a year at his trade could expect to survive an average of only nine weeks before getting arrested. A full-time robber would be arrested, on the average, after eight weeks. For that long a period to elapse before an arrest, the take in the average unreported crime would have to be as great as in the reported crimes, an unlikely proposition. It is when the loss is smallest that reporting of it is least frequent. For those burglars and robbers also trying to support drug habits, $10,000 a year would not carry them very far. They would have to commit many more crimes, and their chances of apprehension would rise correspondingly.

In this brief cost-benefit analysis, I have assumed that burglaries and robberies are not the occasional moonlighting work of people otherwise occupied as construction workers, bank tellers, cabdrivers, lawyers, and doctors. They are, instead, the work of people who look to crime as a principal source of livelihood. The chances of early apprehension, I believe, are so great that robbers and burglars are only rarely able to gain enough experience to become very proficient at this way of earning a living. Unfortunately for both the perpetrators of these crimes and the rest of us, the popular myth is that crime pays. "Since so few burglars, rapists and muggers are caught," said a June 30, 1975, *Time* cover story on crime in discussing the proportion of arrests to reported crimes, "the profile of the criminal is hard to draw." For *Time*'s concern to have any validity, one has to assume that people commit a single crime and then no more. This runs counter to both common sense and everything that is known about crime. *Time*'s editors should have been able to figure out, though they didn't, that arrests and convictions tell us exactly who commits crime. The criminals we catch are the same criminals who got away previously but who don't keep getting away indefinitely. If the myth could be dispelled and burglars and robbers knew their chances of apprehension, they might be deterred from committing these crimes.[6]

"Routine patrol" is the most important police function both in shaping public attitudes toward the police and in apprehending criminals. For this reason, I reject the proposal of the President's Commission on Law Enforcement to assign a lower status to people entering departments to serve this function than to the more elite "police agents," whose role would be primarily investigatory. I offer an alternative proposal.

Some people ought to be able to enter police departments in low-level command positions as is possible in the armed forces. To qualify for these low-level command posts, they should be required to secure the equivalent of the training given to prospective military commanders at the service academies. Thereafter, a graduate should be required to perform a year of internship as a patrolman in one police department before obtaining a command position in another police department.

The major purpose this proposal would serve is to bring into command positions people who have not had time to acquire the prevailing mores of a police department while working their way up through the ranks. I believe this would disrupt the patterns of corruption now holding an iron grip on so many police departments. I have less confidence that it would diminish other kinds of police abuses, but the elimination of corruption would be no small gain. Citizen respect for, and cooperation with, the police would be enormously enhanced.

Another valuable result of bringing some people into police departments at a command level would be the attraction this would hold for people who aspire to professional careers. In itself, this could improve the quality of police forces, though I attach less significance to this as a reason for change than the overriding need to disrupt entrenched police corruption.

Recruitment of racial minorities and women also has a significant beneficial impact on police forces. Quite aside from the rights of these groups to employment as police, I advocate their recruitment because of the way they improve police forces. White police behave better toward racial minorities if some of their fellow officers are members of those same minorities. And males behave better in all respects when women are around.

Of the nation's 450,000 police officers, only about 18,000, or 4 percent, are members of racial minorities. At that, they are mostly concentrated in a few departments. New York City and Chicago, which between them account for one police officer out of ten in the country, have a third of the country's minority police. New York City's close to a thousand women police nearly equal the number in all other police forces combined.

Most of the women and many of the minority officers are very recent additions to the New York City Police Department. Police precincts in New York City now also employ women civilians in clerical positions. These used to be filled by male police officers. The presence of women in the station houses has dramatically altered the atmosphere for the better. Ghetto precincts in New York no longer have quite the embattled-fortress atmosphere that previously characterized them.

Elsewhere, women in particular face deeply entrenched prejudices against their capacity to serve as police officers. Philadelphia Police Commissioner Joseph O'Neill says that though he has "no desire to embarrass women, there are, in fact, certain times of the month when a woman is emotionally and physically incapable of doing her work." The inspector in command of policewomen in Philadelphia, Thomas Roselli, adds his view that "opening all the police department jobs to women would be an open invitation to rampant lesbianism within the department." Little wonder, then, that the 86 female officers in Philadelphia (as contrasted with 8,276 males) are all assigned to the juvenile division. When Officer Penny Brace, a policewoman in Philadelphia since 1965, applied for corporal or detective classification, she was turned down because "you are not a policeman."

The courts are beginning to force police departments to add more members of racial minorities and may also play a part in forcing the addition of women. Federal law requires the Law Enforcement Assistance Administration to deny funds to police departments discriminating on grounds of race and sex, and the most promising legal attack may be an ACLU lawsuit demanding that the LEAA comply with the law and use its economic leverage.

Enforcement of the law is far from the sum and substance of police work. We also rely upon the police to maintain order and to provide a great variety of community services. In the course of a day's work, a police officer may settle a family argument, give first aid to an injured person, summon an ambulance, cordon off a street, help firemen to fight a blaze, quiet noisy neighbors, give directions to people who have gotten lost, and help a blind man cross a street. These duties may consume far more of his time than efforts specifically directed toward preventing crime or apprehending criminals. By providing such services, police should be able to obtain in return the cooperation of citizens to aid them in their crime-control work. But mistrust of the police is pervasive in large segments of the population despite their reliance on the police for a host of important services. It cannot be alleviated by public-relations campaigns. The solution lies in discovering the cause of the mistrust and rooting it out.

The cause, I believe, is police corruption. While entry into police forces at the command level and diversification of recruitment could do a great deal to mitigate corruption, I do not claim it would be entirely eliminated. There is something in the very nature of police work that breeds dishonesty. Police see the worst side of human behavior. It would be hard for them not to become extreme cynics about their fellow human beings and not to be corrupted by what goes on around them.

Police commanders must constantly combat corruption if there is to be any chance of keeping it out of their departments. Yet one can hardly expect a commander to challenge corrupt practices if he has to partake in them or blink at them to achieve his position.

7

Random Law Enforcement: The Serendipity Theory

An officer of a local police department in Arkansas stopped a man driving a late model Ford automobile bearing Texas registration. An inquiry of NCIC via Arkansas' Criminal Justice and Highway Safety Information Center on the vehicle identification number disclosed that the vehicle had been stolen in Rhode Island a year ago.

In Daytona Beach, Florida, recently a man wanted in a fraud case in California ended up in double trouble when he discovered that the man whose identification he was carrying was also wanted. Volusia County Sheriff's deputies stopped two suspicious looking hitchhikers and made inquiries of the Florida Crime Information Center (FCIC) based on the identification they were carrying. One of the inquiries hit a wanted person record of a man being sought by the local police in connection with a hit-and-run accident.

Officers of Morristown Police Department, Tennessee, while on patrol stopped a vehicle, bearing one Indiana license plate, for running a red light. An inquiry of NCIC via the Tennessee Information Enforcement System (TIES) on the license plate indicated it had not been

86

reported stolen. However, a check of the vehicle identification number resulted in a hit on a vehicle that had been stolen two months prior in Indiana.

These are "hits on the system" reported in recent issues of the National Crime Information Center (NCIC) newsletter. They are typical of the random stops and checks now relied upon by police as a major method of apprehending criminals. I believe it should be called the serendipity theory of law enforcement. Here is how it works.

Police seek as many opportunities as possible to stop people and check their identities. A name so obtained is then radioed to one of ninety terminals across the country. From there, it is checked by computer with the FBI's National Crime Information Center. The information from the NCIC is then radioed to the police officer. The entire transaction is completed in a matter of seconds.

The first plans for a National Crime Information Center were announced by J. Edgar Hoover in 1965. He sought no specific legislative authority. A law passed by Congress in 1930, authorizing the FBI to exchange criminal records with state agencies, provided Hoover with all the statutory authority he thought he needed. The NCIC would "mean no intrusion whatsoever upon the right to privacy," Hoover assured Americans. Rather, it would offer protection for "the average, law-abiding citizen."

The NCIC began operating in 1967. At the time, only fifteen police agencies were hooked into the system. It remained experimental until December 1970 when Attorney General John Mitchell resolved a dispute over control of the NCIC by giving the FBI the go-ahead to construct the system. Today, more than six thousand police departments across the country are linked by computer with the NCIC.

The NCIC stores identifying data on people wanted on criminal charges and on stolen vehicles, guns, and other identifiable stolen property. As of April 1, 1975, there were 5,170,631 active records in the NCIC. Of this total, 152,541 were of wanted persons. Another 565,159 records were histories of the criminal records of persons not wanted for any crime at that moment. These computerized criminal histories can be used by police who happen to stop those people to help them determine whether to investigate further. After all, a person with a criminal history might be up to something, even if he isn't wanted on any particular charge at the moment of police contact. The remainder of the records in the NCIC system were of stolen property.

During March 1975, the NCIC averaged 186,038 transactions a day—a total of 5,767,178 for that month. At that rate, the NCIC should engage in close to 70 million transactions during the course of a year. Each transaction is an opportunity to check a person, a license plate, or some other property with the NCIC to see if a "hit" can be made.

During the course of a year, checks with the NCIC are likely to result in about half a million hits. That is a very large number. It is large, that is, until one realizes that it takes about 69.5 million misses to obtain half a million hits. More than 99 percent of the people stopped for interrogation by the police in their efforts to obtain hits are innocent victims of random law enforcement.

The Supreme Court of the United States has done everything it can to legitimize guesswork, serendipitous law enforcement. In a 1969 decision in the case of *Terry* v. *Ohio,* the Supreme Court upheld "stop-and-frisk" laws. These laws permit police to approach a person who looks "suspicious," [1] demand identification from the person and an explanation of his activities. They also allow police to pat down the person to see if he has a weapon. It is the identity check that now triggers the effort to get an NCIC hit. With less than one chance in a hundred of success, of course, police have to stop and frisk a great many people to come up with a significant number of hits.

The full brunt of law enforcement by serendipity falls on the nation's 110 million motorists. It used to be that a police car would stop a person for a traffic violation and the officer would stand next to the driver while writing a ticket. No longer. The police officer returns to his own car and radios the name of the driver and the automobile license number to the NCIC. The reason a particular motorist is stopped may have less to do with the traffic violation than with such characteristics as race, youth, and hair length, which correlate in the police officer's mind with the probability of an NCIC hit.

Police have sought other dividends from their power to stop motorists, and the Supreme Court has accommodated them. In a late 1973 decision, the Court upheld the right of a police officer to search people arrested for traffic violations. The case before the Court involved a man named Robinson driving an old car in Washington, D.C. A police officer recognized Robinson as someone previously found driving after his operator's permit was revoked. Robinson was ordered to stop, got out of the car, and was told he was under arrest for "operating after revocation and obtaining a permit by misrepresentation." The officer searched Robinson, found a crumpled-up cigarette packet in Robinson's pocket, examined its contents, and found heroin. The Supreme Court upheld the legality of the search.

State laws permit police officers to arrest motorists on a great variety of charges. Drivers can be arrested for speeding or for just about any other traffic violation. Prior to the *Robinson* case, a police officer's decision as to whether to make an arrest for an offense of lesser significance than drunk driving would usually turn on whether a motorist had a proper license and registration papers in his possession. Now an arrest legitimizes a full search. If the officer wants an opportunity to try to find some contraband on the driver or in the car, he has incentive to make an arrest. Thereafter, anything he finds in a search is admissible in evidence in a criminal prosecution of the driver.

In other recent decisions, the Supreme Court also said it was all right for a policeman to approach a person sitting in a parked car, reach in, and frisk the person on the basis of an uncorroborated tip from an unnamed informer. If police stop a car because a headlight is out, they can ask for "consent" to search the entire car. The Supreme Court now says the police officer doesn't have to tell a motorist of his absolute right to refuse consent.

If the police arrest a motorist on a traffic violation and take him to a station house, and the motorist's fingerprints are taken when he is booked—as they will be—a check of the prints with a state criminal records data bank or the FBI may disclose that the driver gave the police a false name. The person's true identity revealed, police may discover they have made a hit. The ability to check fingerprints enhances the attraction of making arrests. The reason for the arrest doesn't much matter. What matters is its utility in triggering a more sophisticated identity check than is possible with just the name on a person's driver's license or the license plate on a car. Or so the theory goes.

When people are arrested, their fingerprints are shipped to the FBI's Identification Division, an older, slower, but much more inclusive data bank than the computerized National Crime Information Center. According to the Annual Report of the Attorney General of the United States for 1973, the Identification Division had 159,345,941 fingerprint cards on file.[2] This has several advantages for law-enforcement agencies. They find out more about the person than they could from the NCIC. Interesting information may turn up to use against the person. The arrest adds a set of fingerprints to the Identification Division that may not yet be on file. These prints can be used to check the person's background at some later date when he may apply for public employment, the kind of private employment that is cleared through the Identification Division, or a license to practice a particular trade. And, of course, after the _Robinson_ decision, no matter what the reason for the arrest, a full search is legitimate.

These are among the consequences of serendipitous law enforcement against motorists: In 1971, according to FBI estimates, there were 644,100 arrests for driving under the influence of liquor. By 1973, the number had risen to 946,800, an increase of 47 percent in just two years. Marijuana arrests, most of which involve motorists, went up even more sharply, from 225,878 in 1971 to 420,700 in 1973.

Drunk driving is a very serious crime. It kills a lot of people. Possession of marijuana should not be a crime. Both crimes allow police to arrest drivers, obtain thorough checks of their identities, enter them in the system with arrest records, and search them and their cars. As noted earlier drunk driving probably did not increase between 1971 and 1973 in the spectacular fashion suggested by a 47 percent increase in arrests. As for marijuana, though arrests for its use had been rising sharply since the mid-1960s, even the police were becoming aware of its triviality by the early 1970s. But concern about whether these offenses were more prevalent misses the point. Insofar as drunk driving is concerned, only the arrests were more frequent. It is almost immaterial to police whether arrests are followed by convictions. Police investigatory purposes are completed when arrests take place.

In early 1975, Frances Knight, the veteran director of the State Department's Passport Office, proposed that all American citizens be required to carry identification cards issued by the Federal government. She said it would help the fight against crime. The suggestion was vigorously denounced in statements by civil liberties spokesmen, legislators, and newspaper editorial writers. It was likened to the passbook system in South Africa and the internal passports in the Soviet Union.

The difficulty with both Ms. Knight's proposal and the denunciations is that they missed the same point: With the blessing of the United States Supreme Court, something approaching a universal law-enforcement identity system is actually coming into being. The NCIC provides instantaneous checks of automobile license plates and names on drivers' licenses. "Stop-and-frisk" laws sweep into the system poor people of the sort who live in ghettos and do not drive cars. And arrests are the device for further identity checks when a police officer is not content with the NCIC report alone.

The benefits they derive from enforcement of the traffic laws have stimulated police to react negatively to periodic suggestions such as the proposal offered by the President's Commission on Law Enforcement that this portion of police work be turned over to less highly trained and lower salaried persons. Only a handful of communities have "meter maids," and where they are employed they are limited to enforcement of parking regulations. Since this does not engage them in confrontations with motorists, it provides no opportunity for identity checks or searches of the sort police can engage in when they stop motorists for moving violations.

Law enforcement by serendipity gets results. Thousands of fugitives are apprehended. Stolen goods are occasionally discovered by searches incidental to arrests for driving under the influence, though not nearly so often as illegal drugs. Even a notorious fugitive on the FBI's most-wanted list might be apprehended by a routine check with the National Crime Information Center.

Police in Houston, Texas, scored one such lucky hit in July 1975. A man checked into a hospital for treatment of superficial shotgun wounds. A policeman on duty in the hospital emergency room ran the name he had given, Bradley S. Bruce, through the NCIC computer, and was advised that it was one of the aliases for Thero Wheeler, one of four known surviving members of the Symbionese Liberation Army (SLA) still at large.[3] The NCIC description of Thero Wheeler matched the man who had identified himself as Bradley S. Bruce. He was arrested and charged with escape from the California State Prison at Vaccaville, where he had been serving a sentence for assaulting a police officer.

To get an occasional Thero Wheeler, some car thieves, and miscellaneous fugitives, police must check out more than a hundred of J. Edgar Hoover's "average law-abiding citizens" for every hit. A lot of the hits on the system are for crimes I would abolish, principally drug possession. To permit full identity checks and searches, millions of people must acquire arrest records. And tens of millions of persons must endure stops-and-frisks and traffic stops so our police can add to their number of transactions with the National Crime Information Center and maximize their chances for "hits on the system." While we weren't paying attention, we acquired a passbook system.

Are the results worth it? I doubt it.

8
Incorrigible Children

More than 600,000 children are arrested each year for conduct that would not be criminal if they were adults.

Mrs. Mercale (not her real name) did not have much use for her daughter Maria. The child interfered with her mother's work as a part-time prostitute. Maria spent the first seven years of her life in foster care. Thereafter, she lived with her grandmother, only rarely spending time with her mother. When Maria was twelve, Mrs. Mercale filed a PINS petition against her daughter. The PINS petition charged Maria with being truant from school for several days. It also said Maria was "disruptive in the home" and refused "to obey the directions given her by the [mother] in matters relating generally to her welfare."

PINS stands for "*Person In Need of Supervision.*" Under New York State law, PINS "means a male less than sixteen years of age and a female less than eighteen years of age who does not attend school in accord with the provisions of part one of article sixty-five of the education law or who is incorrigible, ungovernable, or habitually disobedient and beyond the lawful control of parent or other lawful authority." Similar laws exist in every state. They are known as CHINS, CINS, JINS, or MINS laws—for Child, Juvenile, or *Minor In Need* of Supervision.

94

A family court in Brooklyn considered the PINS charge against Maria. While its proceedings were under way, she was held in a jail for children, the "juvenile center." Maria spent more than three months there. Eventually she was convicted as a PINS and put on probation. Maria went back to live with her grandmother. Some months later, Mrs. Mercale, who still did not live with her daughter, filed a "violation of probation," charging Maria with arguing with neighbors, begging cigarettes on the street, and "not obeying the lawful commands of the [mother]." The court revoked probation and put Maria in the custody of the Commissioner of Social Services of the City of New York.

The commissioner put Maria in Callagy Hall, a shelter for neglected children. Maria ran away to return to her grandmother. Callagy Hall filed a new PINS petition. It said Maria was incorrigible because of the earlier PINS petitions filed by Mrs. Mercale and because she ran away from Callagy to her grandmother's home. The family court again declared Maria a PINS and sentenced her to eighteen months in the New York State Training School at Hudson. Thereafter, the court extended her stay for another year. At the age of sixteen, she was paroled on condition she live with her mother. Maria's grandmother had moved to Puerto Rico. Except for four months in Bellevue Hospital's psychiatric ward, Maria has since lived with her mother.

Of the 600,000 children arrested each year for offenses that would not be crimes if they were committed by adults, about 200,000 spend some time confined in jails. Most such jails are exclusively for children, like the juvenile center where Maria was initially confined. In some communities, "incorrigible" children are confined in jails with adult criminals. About 85,000 children a year are sent to long-term "correctional" institutions. Of these children, 23 percent of the boys and 70 percent of the girls are found guilty of offenses that would not be crimes if committed by adults.

Among Maria Mercale's fellow PINS inmates in New York

State training schools, 24 percent were there because they had been labeled as truants; 24 percent for running away from home; 21 percent, like Maria, were there because of "refusal to obey"; 10 percent were in training schools for "staying out late"; 6 percent for "associating with bad companions"; 2 percent for "vile language"; 2 percent for "intoxication and glue sniffing"; and 1 percent for "sexual misconduct." The remaining 10 percent were originally charged with violations of the law that would also be criminal for adults, many of them as violators of the drug laws. The criminal charges against them were "reduced" to PINS.

Locking up PINS children for "associating with bad companions" has a special irony. Except in a few places where it is forbidden by statute or court order, PINS children are herded into the same institutions as children who have committed murder, rape, and robbery. In some places, there are no separate juvenile-detention facilities. Children awaiting trial are put in adult jails. If they associated with bad companions outside, think of their companions in jails and training schools!

Girls commit comparatively few real crimes. But most of the PINS cases involving "staying out late" and "sexual misconduct" are brought against girls. A recent law-review article noted:

Sexual delinquency is by far the most common reason for young women coming into contact with police or courts. Charges such as incorrigibility and ungovernability are merely euphemisms for sexual misconduct. To the extent that male juveniles go unpunished for similar behavior, the vague language incorporated within sex-neutral juvenile morals statutes permits discriminatory enforcement of different sexual standards for males and females.[1]

This discriminatory enforcement accounts for the disproportionate number of girls incarcerated as PINS.

Susan Farmer (not her real name) was sent to a training school because of sexual misconduct. She had a very troubled childhood. From the time she was seven, her mother lived with a man who was drunk more often than not. He made sexual advances toward Susan and her sisters, including a mentally retarded sister. Susan took to staying away from home as much as possible. When she was thirteen, she tried to commit suicide and had to be hospitalized for a month.

When she was fourteen, Susan's mother filed a PINS petition against her. The charges were staying away from home and having sexual relations with a boy her own age. She spent six months in a juvenile-detention center and, after trial, was placed on probation. When Susan violated probation a second time, she was sent to a training school for eighteen months.

The earliest versions of contemporary training schools were the houses of refuge opened in New York, Boston, and Philadelphia in the 1820s. As in the case of the prisons and mental hospitals founded at about the same time, the houses of refuge were thought to be helpful to their inmates. Institutionalization would separate children from an environment that made them disobedient and unruly.

Because the houses of refuge, or reformatories, were perceived as benevolent institutions, it didn't much matter how children got into them. Sometimes courts would commit children to these institutions. Other times they would simply be turned over by parents or by public officials. Children convicted of minor crimes, neglected and abused children, and children who had run away from home mingled with each other in the houses of refuge.

Many of the institutions founded in the early part of the nineteenth century had deteriorated badly by the 1880s and 1890s. They were dirty and overcrowded. Elmira Reformatory, a bellwether institution, had 1,500 inmates in the 1890s instead of the 500 it was designed to hold. The times were ripe for a new reform movement.

The reformers of the late nineteenth century were different from their predecessors in one major respect: They included a significant number of women. It was a time of emerging feminism.

Graduates of the colleges for women founded in the mid-nineteenth century were eager to get out of the home and play a role in public affairs. It wasn't easy. They couldn't vote and therefore had no weight in politics. There were very few paid jobs befitting upper-class, well-educated women. Volunteer work for social welfare was just about all that remained open to them.

Antifeminists resisted any public-affairs role for women. With this exception: Antifeminists could agree that women should take charge of efforts to help children. "Child-saving," criminologist Anthony Platt points out, "was a reputable task for any woman who wanted to extend her housekeeping functions into the community without denying anti-feminist stereotypes of woman's nature and place." [2]

Jane Addams and the other upper-class women who labored so diligently on behalf of children in the 1880s and 1890s did much good in improving the conditions of jails and reformatories. In the process, however, they enlarged state control over children in ways that reflected their own values. They were horrified to find children hanging around billiard parlors, taverns, theaters, and dance halls. Sexual promiscuity appalled them. As affluent women who enjoyed country homes, they wanted to take children away from the corrupting environment of the city to the sylvan surroundings they knew and loved. A training school or reformatory in the countryside seemed to them a far better place for a child to grow up than an urban slum.

The mechanism for extending state control over children was the juvenile court. Illinois, Jane Addams's state, passed the first Juvenile Court Act in 1899. Over the next twenty years, similar laws were passed by virtually every other state. These laws viewed children as objects for benevolent treatment rather than as small adults some of whom had committed crimes and some of whom were innocent. Juvenile courts blurred such distinctions. A child who had committed no crime might still be in danger of becoming delinquent and should be protected by the benevolent intervention of the juvenile court. On the other hand, a child who had committed a very serious crime was still a child and could yet be saved.

The language of the juvenile court helps blur the distinction between crime and status. As the President's Commission on Law Enforcement pointed out, juvenile courts talk about

Petition instead of complaint, summons instead of warrant, initial hearing instead of arraignment, finding of involvement instead of conviction, disposition instead of sentence. . . .The goals were to investigate, diagnose, and prescribe treatment, not to adjudicate guilt or fix blame. The individual's background was more important than the facts of a given incident, specific conduct relevant more as symptomatic of a need for the court to bring its helping powers to bear than as prerequisite to exercise of jurisdiction. Lawyers were unnecessary—adversary tactics were out of place, for the mutual aim of all was not to contest or object but to determine the treatment plan best for the child. That plan was to be devised by the increasingly popular psychologists and psychiatrists; delinquency was thought of almost as a disease, to be diagnosed by specialists and the patient kindly but firmly dosed.[3]

To Roscoe Pound, the juvenile court was one of the great social legacies of the nineteenth century. It was the fulfillment of a noble dream. "What we did not have," an early juvenile-court judge said of the period before his court existed, "was the conception that a child that broke the law was to be dealt with by the State as a wise parent would deal with a wayward child." The juvenile court could save children from delinquency, its champions claimed, by timely intervention in their lives. If a child did go astray, the juvenile court could set the child back on the right path through gentle treatment.

The noble dream has had some bizarre consequences. In New York State, a fourteen- or fifteen-year-old who commits murder or rape can be sentenced to a state training school for a maximum of eighteen months. This is the sentence Maria Mercale served for disobeying her mother, and the sentence served by Susan Farmer for having sexual relations with a boy her own age. Worse, in practice, PINS children serve sentences four to five months longer than children who have committed real crimes. As a result, the majority of children locked up are in juvenile prisons because they are in need of supervision rather than because they have committed acts that would not be crimes if committed by adults.

The language of deception hides the treatment of the 65,000 to 70,000 children incarcerated in long-term detention facilities. "Training school" substitutes for "prison," "child-care worker" for "guard," "campus" for "prison grounds," and "cottage" for "cell block." It doesn't sound so bad when incorrigible children are remanded to treatment by child-care workers and live in cottages on a campus. An altogether different effect comes from saying a truant gets sentenced to a prison, lives in a cell, and is in the custody of juvenile-prison guards.[4]

Any arguments in favor of juvenile prison for status offenders and of juvenile-court practices must rest on the results they have achieved. Is it true that the court's early intervention in a child's life prevents later criminal behavior? The evidence suggests just the opposite. Studies in the 1930s and 1940s by psychologists and sociologists such as Sheldon and Eleanor Glueck, Clifford Shaw, and Henry D. McKay demonstrated very high rates of subsequent arrest for real crimes of children who had spent time in training schools. These institutions readied children for criminal careers as adults. Later studies confirmed these findings.

Summarizing the available research for the President's Commission on Law Enforcement, sociologist Edwin Lemert pointed out, "They demand explanation as to why the large population of youth committing delinquent acts and made court wards commit more rather than fewer delinquencies. The conclusion that the court processing rather than the behavior in some way helps to fix and perpetuate delinquency in many cases is hard to escape."[5]

In the most comprehensive recent study of delinquency, three prominent sociologists studied the lives of all boys born in

Philadelphia in 1945. Of nearly 10,000 boys in the "cohort," 35 percent had one or more contacts with police between their tenth and eighteenth birthdays. Some cases were "adjusted" informally; some boys were arrested and had the charges against them dismissed; some were punished by courts, either by sentences of probation or incarceration. In determining the treatment a youngster would get, race proved of greater significance than any other factor, including seriousness of the offense and previous history of delinquency.

Not only do a greater number of those who receive punitive treatment (institutionalization, fine or probation) continue to violate the law, but they also commit more serious crimes with greater rapidity than those who experience a less constraining contact with the judicial and correctional systems [the sociologists discovered]. Thus, we must conclude that the juvenile justice system, at its best, has no effect on the subsequent behavior of adolescent boys and, at its worst, has a deleterious effect on future behavior.[6]

One possible reason the juvenile court increases delinquency is the stigma with which it burdens a child. In theory, this is something juvenile courts try to avoid. Most state laws governing juvenile-court operations claim to make their records confidential. In practice, confidentiality is virtually nonexistent. The records are made available to the FBI, the armed services, civil service agencies, and local police agencies. Any of these agencies may circulate the records farther. They handicap youths when they apply for jobs, licenses, school admissions, or entry into the armed forces.

Even if the records were kept confidential, the problem of stigma would persist. If a fourteen-year-old spends three months in a juvenile-detention center or eighteen months in a training school, the absence will have to be explained when the child attempts to reenter school. The child will also lose ground in schoolwork during the period of incarceration. Rather than face the embarrassment, a child may choose to avoid school. The absence and its reasons will also be known to family, neighbors, and friends. It may establish or confirm their view of the child as a "bad boy" or "bad girl."

When children commit real crimes—murder, rape, or robbery—these stigmatizing consequences of court processing are unavoidable. Courts must punish these acts by children for the same reason they must punish adults. Some children, as well as adults, commit crimes so grotesque they should be held in prison to protect other people for the period they are incarcerated. Low-level punishment is an appropriate response to lesser crimes by children. Larceny, often in the form of shoplifting, is the most characteristic juvenile crime that would also be a crime if committed by someone older. It should be punished by probation, and, if it is repetitive, by brief confinement as a last resort. The studies demonstrating that confinement increases criminality dictate very parsimonious use of prison for children.

Demands have been growing for the restriction of juvenile-court jurisdiction. Some of the demands come from people who want to stop "coddling" children. To a lesser extent, the demands come from people who want to stop the state from coercive interference in the lives of children who have committed status offenses but have done nothing that would also be criminal if done by an adult.

In a neat historical reversal, an organization of well-educated and well-to-do women concerned with social welfare, the successors of the "child savers" of the nineteenth century, is now a leader in the effort to eliminate PINS jurisdiction. Three thousand volunteers from the National Council of Jewish Women (NCJW) have been gathering information on the way children are abused as PINS. One of the NCJW observers reported on a fourteen-year-old boy led from home in handcuffs. His parents complained he was out of control. Later on, it turned out his disobedience consisted of refusal to take a bath. Other observers visited a "showcase" training school. A thirteen-year-old boy was instructed by a staff person, "Show the ladies how we shine floors." "Head bowed," the observers reported, "the boy slipped a square of carpeting under one foot and began shuffling it back and forth." The boy was in the training school because of truancy.

The women compiling these reports are as determined to limit juvenile-court jurisdiction as the women of Jane Addams's generation were to create it. Juvenile judges, still steeped in the nineteenth-century philosophy that created their court, fear a conspiracy between those opponents who want to be tougher on children and those who want to abolish PINS offenses. "Someone is orchestrating what is going to happen in our courts," the chief judge of the Rhode Island Family Court complained early in 1975 at a meeting sponsored by the National College of Juvenile Judges.

The judges are fighting back. A thoughtful and compassionate judge of the civil court in New York, Hortense W. Gabel, wrote an article for *The New York Times* based on her experience as an acting judge of the family court. She described the case of John K., age fourteen. Judge Gabel found he had committed the crimes of possession of a dangerous weapon and attempted sodomy of an eight-year-old boy. She committed John K. to a state training school for the maximum allowable eighteen months.

Well before he came before Judge Gabel, John K.'s life had been filled with problems. He had been referred for a psychiatric examination by the time he was seven and a neurological examination by the time he was eight. He was first arrested at the age of ten. The complaint, a charge of auto theft, was dropped. The case was "adjusted" by the probation department. When he was eleven, John K. was arrested for burglarizing a paint company. He was paroled in his mother's custody. A few months later, he was labeled a PINS. He was placed on probation with a requirement of therapy, but as a result of a mental-health report, was sent to a training school. From there, John K. was transferred to another training school, and, eventually, was sent to a mental hospital. He stayed there for twenty-two months. Shortly after release from the mental hospital, John K. was arrested for menacing his sister with a deadly weapon. Again, community therapy was prescribed. Shortly after that, John K. was arrested on the charges that brought him before Judge Gabel.

It is a depressing story. Unhappily, it is not unique. We have to figure out what to do with children like John K. Judge Gabel bemoans the existence of a "knowledge gap" in dealing with such cases. This is how she describes it:

Information banks are incomplete, inaccurate and mislead the very agencies that are required to understand and act on the development histories of these youngsters, even though it is technologically feasible to organize such banks.

There are no valid psycho-social indicators that can facilitate early identification and treatment of violence-prone children. There is a crying need for such research and identification.

Moreover, there is no evidence that treatment of these young people, in the absence of identification and treatment of the family constellation, will prevent recidivism.

Even if we had many of the necessary diagnostic and treatment tools, we have no sanctions to compel treatment and assistance for the youngsters together with their families.

Judge Gabel concludes:

I believe we are faced with only two options. We can lock the John K.s up until the fires of their youthful violence are banked—in some cases for a lifetime. Or we can reject this grim choice and commit the necessary funds and talent to the researching of knowledge and the drastic institutional change that will be necessary to save these children and rescue our social order.[7]

As these choices are described to us, it is meant to be clear that the more humanitarian thing to do is overcome the knowledge gap identified by Judge Gabel and bring about the drastic institutional change she proposes as an alternative. I disagree.

Judge Gabel and the defenders of the juvenile court would take us farther down the same path we have traveled for the last century. The juvenile court, through its PINS jurisdiction, was supposed to identify children before they committed real crimes and divert them from delinquency. As Judge Gabel sees it, that is too late. The logical consequence of her call for "early identification" is something like the predelinquency testing programs now popular in California, or the Rorschach testing of six- and seven-year-olds proposed by Dr. Arnold Hutschneker to detect the violence-prone. Then there is the question of what to do with these very young children once they are identified. Should they be sent to special camps as Hutschneker proposes? Should they be committed to psychiatric hospitals? John K. had outpatient treatment at one psychiatric hospital and spent twenty-two months in another. Should he have spent the years from six to eight in a mental hospital instead of the years from twelve to fourteen? Or, perhaps, the years from two to four?

Judge Gabel proposes information banks to house the data collected on very young children. If pressed, I am sure she would advocate careful controls on access to this data. Who should see it? Judges? Of course. Probation agencies, police departments, psychiatric hospitals, schools, welfare workers? Yes, probably they should, too. After all, they have to deal with the John K.s of this world. If it is available to all those people, can any limits be placed on its dissemination? Not if the history of family-court records is any guide. The laws making those records confidential have not prevented their promiscuous availability.

Judge Gabel wants to treat "the family constellation" and not just the child. To make this possible, she thinks we will need "sanctions to compel treatment and assistance for the youngsters together with their families." What would these sanctions be? Would she lock up some children as PINS and some parents as P-PINS—Parents of Persons In Need of Supervision? What alternate sanctions? Fines? Reduction of welfare payments? What good would come of any of these sanctions?

I believe there are some things the state should have done to try to prevent the problems of John K. According to Judge Gabel, he was one of six children. His mother had asthma and heart trouble and could not control her children. His father, an alcoholic, disappeared when John K. was very young. Perhaps the state should have paid for a "homemaker" or "mother's helper" to visit Mrs. K. daily, at her option, and help her control the children. It would cost a lot of money, but so does dealing with John K. Judge Gabel informs us it cost $20,000 a year to keep John K. in the psychiatric hospital where he spent two years. It will cost more than $15,000 a year to hold John K. in the training school to which Judge Gabel sent him. All John K.'s other scrapes cost money, too, not to mention the cost to the eight-year-old boy John K. attempted to sodomize.

Describing California's predelinquency programs, Harriet Katz Berman observes that "while it is no news that poverty correlates with crime, none of the projects which used low family income as a selection factor tried altering that factor as a method of intervention." [8] Perhaps homemakers and direct income subvention seem too much like rewards to people for being in trouble. They offend our vestigial Puritan instincts. But they may be a lot cheaper than the treatment given John K. or the even earlier intervention in his life proposed by Judge Gabel.

I have no great confidence that John K.'s criminal behavior could have been prevented if the state had aided Mrs. K. with a "homemaker" or "mother's helper." But it would probably have done some good, and, unless sanctions were attached, it is hard to see what harm it would have done. Judge Gabel's proposals, by contrast, would do a great deal of harm. They reinforce the philosophy of the juvenile court and extend its reach over children who have not committed crimes, insisting that the only reason the court's practices haven't worked is that they haven't gone far enough.

Ultimately, some children, like John K., will commit serious crimes. The well-intentioned juvenile court, with its brief sentences for serious crimes, will not do much good for these children. They will get out of prison after a few months, commit more crimes, and go back to prison again. The "grim choice" of extended imprisonment for them will have to be faced.

And what of the runaways? Of all status offenders in juvenile-court jurisdiction, these present the most serious problems. They can get into a lot of trouble. What is to be done with them? Here, too, some choices must be made.

Each year some 600,000 teenagers leave home. Most don't run very far. They stay in the vicinity of their own homes, often with a friend or relative. The great majority return home on their own in two or three weeks. Some 265,000 runaways are arrested or detained by police in the course of a year. Some, such as Karen Baxter, get into even worse trouble.

Karen, her five brothers and sisters, and her parents lived in a five-room apartment in a run-down Cambridge, Massachusetts, housing project. Mr. Baxter was unemployed, and the family lived on welfare. In the fall of 1974, Karen started high school in Cambridge, but she was frequently truant. In December 1974, her repeated truancy led to a court proceeding.

The court decided Karen could no longer live at home. She would be given a choice. Either she would have to live with a grandmother in Ashby, Massachusetts, or she would be put in a juvenile-detention center. Neither alternative was acceptable to Karen. At the age of fifteen, she ran away to New York City.

In New York, Karen called herself Carol Blake. She became a prostitute, acquired a pimp, and moved into a hotel with him. She was arrested once, but, in the usual fashion with prostitution arrests in New York City, she was released a few hours later. In February 1975, two months after she ran away from home, Karen picked up a customer who murdered her in the hotel room where they had registered as Mr. and Mrs. Smith.

Cases such as Karen Baxter's, which attracted extensive news coverage, are cited by juvenile courts as the reason for interfering in the lives of runaways. The children have to be protected. But in

Karen's case, if a juvenile court had refrained from interfering in her life, she might be alive today. She ran away from the alternatives a court offered her after labeling her as a PINS for truancy.

If runaway children are very young, the state should return them to their parents. If they run away again, they should be returned again, unless, of course, the parents have grossly abused them. Then the state should try to remove children from their parents and place them in adoptive homes. Older runaways, fourteen and fifteen years old, should have places where they can go to live. They should be offered the chance to return to their families, but they should not be forced to go. If they choose to leave one runaway center, they should be free to do so. They might go on to another runaway center, they might not. Some children will get hurt. But it is hardly justifiable for the state to hurt them by incarcerating them as PINS in the guise of protecting them from injury.

The Department of Health, Education and Welfare is now financing runaway centers. About eighty are in operation. Among them, however, they can house only 2,000 or 3,000 children, not nearly enough room to accommodate the great numbers of children on the run. Runaway centers provide safety, shelter, food, and medical attention for children for what are often short periods until the child decides to go home. When the child is ready to go home, the centers make contact with the parents and ease the return. Runaway centers are a cheaper and better alternative for dealing with the problem than PINS jurisdiction.

Truants, "incorrigible" children, and others now labeled PINS present lesser problems of safety than runaways. Perhaps the state's best response to these problems is to do nothing. My advocacy of a hands-off policy does not mean I underestimate the seriousness of the problem. It simply means I think the state, here as elsewhere, does more harm than good by intervening and that these forms of conduct do not justify a punitive response by the state. Whatever the good intentions of the people who gave us our system of juvenile justice, PINS jurisdiction is terribly punitive to those who have committed no crimes, even while the juvenile court is often too lenient with those who have committed serious crimes.

9

Public Responsibility for the Roots of Crime

Larry "Child" was born in 1962. His brother George was born a year later. In November 1963, the New York City Bureau of Child Guidance obtained custody of the two infants. Larry and George never saw their parents again. Their parents' whereabouts are unknown.

In the more than eleven years since New York City obtained custody of them, no permanent home has been found for George and Larry. They have been passed from agency to agency. At various times they have been the responsibility of the New York Foundling Home, Sheltering Arms Children's Services, and Abbott House. They have lived in at least two foster homes, two institutions, and a group home. In one of the foster homes, George and Larry were frequently kept locked up in the basement.

Adoptive homes could probably have been found for George and Larry. But a great many of the private agencies to which the responsibility for these children has been delegated are bogged down in religious and racial matching requirements, arbitrary and irrelevant standards, and their own dependence on the public payments they get while they maintain custody of homeless children. The result: In New York City alone, an estimated 26,000 children like George and Larry lack permanent homes. Across the

110

country, 300,000 children would be a conservative guess. These children are shuttled in and out of institutions and foster homes.

The cause-and-effect relationship between family instability and criminal behavior has been extensively documented by psychologists and sociologists. In their contribution to the report on *Juvenile Delinquency and Youth Crime* for the President's Commission on Law Enforcement, Hyman Rodman and Paul Grams cite more than a hundred studies documenting the connection.[1] It is part of the generally accepted wisdom on the causes of crime. But neither a concern for the crime that results from the lack of a permanent home nor a humanitarian interest in the welfare of the children has prompted any great public interest in the scandalous practices of the child-placement industry.

An investigation of New York City child-care practices by William Heffernan and Stewart Ain, a team of *New York Daily News* reporters, produced the best recent account of the scandal. Among the *News* findings:

—Many child-care agencies, despite claims of poverty, actually have vast resources and investments.

—These same agencies often skimp on food and clothing for children in their institutions and in support payments to foster parents.

—Some agencies falsify records to obtain city payments for children no longer in care.

—The city [New York], despite the fact that it pays $200 million a year to private agencies, makes little effort to determine how many children are being cared for or how the money paid is being spent.

Several child-care experts charged that many children were being denied adoptive homes so that the agencies involved could collect the highest amount possible from the city and thereby assure their own existence. City statistics tend to support that view by showing that in 1974 only 3% of the children found their way into adoptive homes. Some examples:

—Greer, A Children's Community. This agency at Millbrook showed no adoptions in 1974 with 326 children in care.

—Speedwell Services for Children, Inc. A Manhattan-based outfit, it had 4 adoptions in 1974 out of 577 children.

—Cardinal McCloskey School and Home. This White Plains agency reported 5 adoptions in 1974 out of 495 children.

—St. Vincent's Hall. A Brooklyn institution, it listed one adoption in 1974 out of 725 children in care.

City statistics also showed that these same agencies received more than $6 million in 1974 as part of the city's effort to find permanent homes for the children.[2]

New York City, like other cities across the country, pays child-care agencies on a per-child, per-diem basis. In 1973, it cost New York City $12 per child per day for each child in foster care, or $4,380 per child for a year. At that rate, it cost the city about $50,000 for Larry "Child" and a similar amount for his brother George for their more than eleven years in foster care.

A study of the economics of the New York City child-care industry [3] suggests that some of the barriers to adoption would be overcome if the private agencies were given a financial incentive to place children in permanent homes. The authors of the study propose a one-time payment to the agencies of $4,380—the equivalent of the cost for a year in foster care—for each child for whom a private agency finds an adoptive home. At present, New York City pays only $1,400 to agencies for finding permanent homes. This is less than the costs actually incurred by Edwin Gould Services for Children, an agency with an outstanding record of success in placing children for adoption, which could be used as a model for the way private agencies should operate. The suggested payment of $4,380 would be more than adequate to cover the costs of actual placement for adoption, but would still represent an enormous saving to the city if children like Larry and George "Child" were adopted very quickly instead of languishing in foster care for eleven years.[4] Of course, child-care agencies committed to large staffs and substantial overhead costs would still find it more lucrative to keep children in foster care even if the one-time fees for finding permanent homes were more realistic than those prevalent today.

Despite the enormous number of children available for adoption, some people find they must pay large sums of money to adopt children on the "black market." A *New York Daily News* reporter, Lynne McTaggart, investigated the baby market by posing as one-half of a couple who could be expected to have great difficulty in adopting a child. As she described herself to a prominent adoptions lawyer, she was twenty-seven and her husband was fifty-three. That made the husband too old to adopt in the eyes of most adoption agencies. Ms. McTaggart established several other obstacles to her qualifications as an adoptive parent for the investigation: Bernie, her "husband," had three children by an earlier marriage and had had a vasectomy before divorcing his previous wife. Also, she was Catholic, he was Jewish. The couple would have run into difficulties on several grounds. Aside from his age, they would have encountered prejudice against a divorced person, against a person who had sterilized himself, and against parents of different religions. To get a child, Ms. McTaggart and Bernie discovered they would have to pay a black-market fee of $13,000.

In April 1975, the United States Senate Subcommittee on Children and Youth held hearings on baby selling. Witnesses at the hearing from Cleveland, Philadelphia, Los Angeles, and several other cities testified that baby-selling practices in their cities were comparable, and with similar prices, to those encountered by Ms. McTaggart in New York. Couples could not adopt children because of their ages, their income, their religion, or their race. In some states, agencies will not place a child for adoption in a home where the wife works. Almost everywhere, the time it takes to secure a child is so long and the agency's intrusion into the lives of the adoptive parents is so great, they are discouraged from dealing with recognized child-placement agencies. About 5,000 babies are sold on the black market each year, according to the testimony at the Senate hearings by Joseph H. Reid, director of the Child Welfare League of America.

The availability of adoptive homes was also demonstrated by the tremendous demand for the Vietnamese orphans who came to public notice in the closing days of the war in Indochina.

Thousands were placed in just a few days, and still there weren't nearly enough of the children to go around. A couple from Casper, Wyoming, typified the spirit of Americans who adopted Vietnamese orphans. They had two sons of their own, adopted two Vietnamese girls, and got their third Vietnamese girl about the time of the fall of Saigon. The newest child was part black. The husband, a superintendent of a trailer-home company, told *The New York Times* he was worried when his wife first suggested the idea of a racially mixed child, but then accepted the idea. "It makes no difference," he said. "What you're doing is saving a life." 5

Many families dealing with adoption agencies are never informed of the availability of state subsidies to help them meet the costs of adopting a child. Such subsidies, now available in thirty-six states, range from payments to cover medical supplies in some states to as much as $2,000 a year in other states. Unlike foster-care payments, however, these payments are not lucrative sources of income for child-care agencies. Adoption does not require the continuing social work needed for foster care, and therefore adoption subsidies do not include reimbursement of the child-care agency's overhead costs. A family of modest means could be encouraged to adopt a child by awareness of these payments. Instead, families are often dissuaded from adopting children because they are only informed of the $4,000 or more they may be expected to pay even a recognized adoption agency.

The practice of religious matching in adoptions is particularly harmful in New York City, where institutions representing the three major faiths in the city have divided responsibility for the children in need of care. Most black children are entrusted to the care of the Protestant child-care agencies. Most parents in New York seeking children to adopt are Catholic or Jewish. Since some agencies restrict their services and others give preference to their coreligionists, the system of religious matching effectively prevents even larger numbers of black children from being adopted than would otherwise be true.

Failure to find adoptive homes is only one of the ways public policy denies children stable families. Another way is by disrupting families and taking children away from parents who are providing their children with a loving environment.

Charles and Darlene Alsager have six children. They live in a ramshackle house in a working-class section of Des Moines, Iowa. While life was difficult, Charles Alsager managed to earn enough to support his large family without ever requiring public assistance. Family life was the principal pleasure enjoyed by the Alsagers.

Something extraordinary happened to the Alsagers in 1969. A probation officer from the Polk County juvenile court, Jane Johnston, paid an unannounced visit to the Alsager home. Her visit was prompted by complaints from neighbors that the Alsager children pulled up geraniums, broke a swing, and used four-letter words.

Ms. Johnston spent twenty minutes at the Alsager home. She saw dirty dishes in the sink and a good deal of unfolded laundry, clean but strewn about. Like many other homes, no doubt. The Alsagers were poor, and there wasn't much food in the house.

Darlene Alsager and her youngest child, ten-month-old Albert, were alone in the house when Jane Johnston visited. Ms. Johnston and the police officer who accompanied her seized the baby over the protests and tears of the mother. On the way out, Ms. Johnston and the policeman encountered the five older children returning from play. All were swept up and taken to the Polk County Children's Shelter. At this writing, six years later, the Alsagers have just now recovered the four younger children. The children have spent the years in fifteen foster homes and eight juvenile institutions. The Iowa courts upheld the "termination" of the Alsagers as parents, in part because of the complaints about things like pulling up geraniums and in part because a judge decided that the Alsagers were of too low intelligence to give the children proper stimulation. A federal court finally returned the children to their parents just before Christmas 1975.

Ruth R. lives in Brooklyn, New York. Her son Jay, age ten, had problems in school. A school official told Ms. R. that the school was considering suspending Jay. Ms. R. met with members of the staff of the Board of Education's Bureau of Child Guidance to discuss Jay's problem. As a result, Jay was evaluated by a school psychiatrist, who recommended residential treatment for the boy. Ms. R. applied to several residential treatment programs, and Jay was accepted by the Pleasantville Cottage School in Hawthorne, New York, a facility operated by the Jewish Child Care Association. In December 1974, Jay and his mother visited the Pleasantville Cottage School. Jay liked the school and told his mother he would like to go there.

Ms. R. didn't like the looks of the form she was asked to sign to get Jay into the Pleasantville Cottage School. It provided for the "transfer of the care and custody of the child to the Commissioner of Social Services of the City of New York." Could she get Jay back from the custody of the commissioner? A worker from the City Bureau of Child Welfare told her she could, but refused to put the assurance in writing or amend the form to reflect it. When Ms. R. declined to sign the form, she was told Pleasantville wouldn't accept Jay without it. If she didn't sign, the Bureau of Child Welfare might institute a neglect proceeding against Ms. R. in family court and take Jay forcibly.

Ruth R. had a net weekly income of about $115. She couldn't afford to pay for a private residential treatment program. Her suspicions of the form she was asked to sign were well founded. It would give the Commissioner of Social Services in New York City custody of Jay. Thousands of children whose parents sign such forms are not returned. The commissioner retains custody of them even though it was not made clear to the parents they were surrendering their children to the state in exchange for residential treatment.

The LeMays (not their real name), a Virginia couple, got divorced. Both parents wanted custody of their six-year-old son Kevin. They took the quarrel to court. The judge decided to teach a lesson to the disputing parents. He took Kevin away from them both and placed the boy in foster care. Both parents were denied visitation rights for six months.

There had never been any suggestion that either parent had neglected the child.

Also in Virginia, Jane Perkins (not her real name) took her fifteen-day-old baby to a blood bank to wait for her husband Charles while he was giving blood. A welfare official saw Ms. Perkins there with the very young baby and decided the father had probably abandoned the child. He started to question Ms. Perkins. She has a speech defect and had some difficulty responding to his questions. The welfare official jumped to a second erroneous conclusion; he decided Ms. Perkins was mentally retarded. Having by this time persuaded himself that there was no father to care for the child and the mother was incompetent, he simply seized the baby from Ms. Perkins.

Virginia law provides for no hearing either in advance of child seizures or immediately afterward. Charles and Jane Perkins had to go to Federal court to get their baby back.

Estimating the number of children improperly seized from their parents is very difficult. It is surely in the tens of thousands each year, but any closer estimate would be sheer guesswork. Many of the children now languishing in foster care or in child-care institutions were taken away from their parents by an interventionist state in the mistaken belief the state had a better way of protecting children. The "best interests of the child" is the slogan governing public policy on child care. Although it has recently been challenged,[6] it has allowed too easy disruption of relationships between children and their biological parents. When the state intervenes in family affairs, it often makes a good situation bad or an unhappy situation worse.

In my view, state laws should spell out a strong presumption in favor of allowing biological parents to raise their children. Unfitness would have to be proved before children could be taken away, except in emergency circumstances when the child must be removed pending a hearing to prevent severe physical abuse of the child. In an emergency, a hearing would have to be held immediately after removal of the child.

The presumption in favor of the biological parents would be overcome by evidence of abandonment, a degree of neglect amounting to abandonment, or gross physical abuse. A parent's incapacity to care for a child should not be grounds for removal against the wishes of the parent. The state can deal with that problem by providing care within the child's own home.

A child's right to a permanent home should command public support even if it bears no relationship to crime. But given the virtually universal consensus that family instability is a direct cause of crime, the urgency of reforming public policy is all the more dramatic. Ironically, while many social services are denied people because of their cost, child-care policy could probably be reformed at either no great cost to the state or with a reduction in expenditure. It is financially costly to interfere unnecessarily between biological parents and child, and it is costly to keep children in the instability of long-term institutional or foster care. Providing care in the home through nurses and homemakers is not cheap, but it is far less expensive than the alternative now in use. A money-saving social policy is one with a strong bias in favor of keeping or finding permanent homes for children. It would also be a crime-saving and a lifesaving social policy.

10
Public Responsibility for the Roots of Crime:

CONTINUED

Public policy should help families stay together. Public policy should keep children in school. Public policy should try to reduce transiency. But for bureaucratic reasons, public policy does just the opposite. Thereby, it causes crime.

John Morris earns $7,000 a year wrapping packages in a New York City clothing store. The money is not enough to support his family—his wife, a three-year-old daughter, and a two-year-old son. But Mr. Morris (not his real name) has solved his problem. He has moved away from his family. He now lives by himself three blocks away. John Morris's absence from home makes his wife, Nelda Morris, eligible for welfare payments for herself and the two children. They collect about $4,000 a year in cash and are automatically entitled to food stamps and Medicaid. Now that it has split up, the Morris family has virtually doubled its income.

When they first split, John and Nelda continued to see each other almost every day. Their visits were furtive so a welfare worker wouldn't think they were still living together. John Morris gave his wife money and spent a lot of time with the children. After several months, however, the visits became less frequent. Nelda Morris believes John has taken up with another woman, and she doesn't want to see him very often. John Morris rarely has any money to give his wife anymore and sees the children only about

119

once a week, sometimes once every two weeks. He is no longer much of a father to them.

According to the Bureau of the Census, by 1973, 20.7 percent of all households among whites were headed by females without a male present. Among blacks and other racial minorities, the figure was 37.5 percent. The number of households without males has been climbing steadily for several decades. While some small part of the recent growth may be attributable to the influence of the feminist movement, the greatly disproportionate number of female-headed households among the poor suggests other factors are at work. The economic pressures on John and Nelda Morris to split affect far more families than go-it-alone decisions by newly liberated women.

According to a recent study of welfare in New York City, "the data from the welfare mothers themselves reveal that among about a fifth of them, the decision to break up the marriage or relationship was influenced by the availability of welfare; that is welfare was either regarded as a reasonable option or was used as a device to maximize income." [1] The proportion may be even higher elsewhere. Unlike some other states, New York provides general assistance to very poor, intact families. While John Morris earned too much to qualify for welfare payments if he stayed home, the family could have stayed together and still obtained general assistance if he had earned less.

The Federal government finances welfare payments to people in four categories: the aged, the blind, the permanently and totally disabled, and families with dependent children. It does not pay for general assistance to poor people who fall outside these categories. Such general assistance as exists depends on the meager financing the states can provide. One of the criteria for welfare payments to dependent children is that at least one parent be dead, physically or mentally disabled, or away from home. That is why John Morris had to move away from home to enable his family to obtain welfare payments.

Dwight Lopez was one of about seventy-five students suspended by Central High School in Columbus, Ohio, for a lunchroom disturbance. He said he wasn't involved and was only an innocent bystander. That didn't matter. There was never a hearing to determine whether the suspension was justified.

Betty Crome, a student at McGuffy Junior High School in Columbus, was also suspended without a hearing. As the United States Supreme Court stated in a case involving her and Dwight Lopez, Betty Crome's offense was being "present at a demonstration at a high school different from the one she was attending. There she was arrested together with others, taken to the police station, and released without being formally charged. Before she went to school on the following day, she was notified that she had been suspended."

In *Goss* v. *Lopez,* the Supreme Court's January 1975 decision in the case of Dwight Lopez, Betty Crome, and seven other Columbus, Ohio, students, some new principles were established to govern school suspensions. The Court held that a student facing a ten-day suspension from school must be given oral or written notice of the charges against him, and, if the student denies the charges, an explanation of the evidence the authorities have and an opportunity to present his side of the story. These are "rudimentary precautions against unfair or mistaken findings of misconduct and arbitrary exclusion from school," according to the five Justices, appointed prior to the time Richard Nixon became President, who made up the Supreme Court's majority in the case.

The Court went on to say "that we have addressed ourselves solely to the short suspension, not exceeding 10 days. Longer suspensions or expulsions for the remainder of the school term, or permanently, may require more formal procedures." Those more formal procedures could include the right of a child to face his accuser, present his own witnesses, cross-examine witnesses against him, have the assistance of counsel and opportunity for an effective appeal.

A lot of children are affected by the Supreme Court's decision in *Goss* v. *Lopez.* The rules of many school systems and some state laws and state boards of education had previously required due process before children could be suspended or expelled from school. But in much of the country, arbitrary and unreviewable decisions by school administrators, without any stated procedures, determined whether children could attend school. Even where there were laws and rules against this sort of thing, they were widely ignored. One consequence: According to the 1970 census, close to 2 million children between ages seven and seventeen did not attend school at all. Most were out of school because they had been expelled or excluded, not because they wanted to be out of school.

Children are excluded from school for many reasons. Some are mentally or physically handicapped, and schools have no programs for them. Others are alleged to have created disciplinary problems. Expulsion was their punishment. Among girls, pregnancy is a leading cause for expulsion. In some parts of the South, expulsion of black children is used to resegregate schools integrated by court order. A similar enterprise was undertaken a few years ago by a large New York City high school. It expelled 670 black and Puerto Rican children on a single day because turmoil in the school was blamed on "racial imbalance."

The Supreme Court's decision in *Goss* v. *Lopez* does not conclude the struggle to get due process for children before they can be thrown out of school any more than the Supreme Court's decision in *Brown* v. *Board of Education* twenty-one years earlier concluded the struggle to integrate the schools. But the *Lopez* decision establishes some principles countrywide to aid those seeking due process.

The National Education Association (NEA), the largest organization of teachers in the country, provided support for Betty Crome, Dwight Lopez, and their fellow Columbus students in bringing their case to the Supreme Court. For this, the NEA was attacked by Albert Shanker, president of the rival American Federation of Teachers. "Most of America's teachers will believe that the Court was wrong," said Shanker in a February 9, 1975, advertisement in *The New York Times*, paid for by his union. "They will be saddened to find that their task has been made more difficult by the actions of one of their own teacher organizations." Shanker went on:

It is true that some student suspensions have been unfair, but failure to suspend disruptive students is also unfair. Such failure is unfair to all the other students in the class, who are unable to learn because the teacher's time and energy are entirely consumed by one or two children. It is no argument against the basic principle of due process to contend that in this instance it will serve to keep students in school who shouldn't be there; that in protecting the rights of the disruptive child it will sacrifice the rights of all others in his class.

The resistance of Shanker and others who share his views will make it very difficult to ensure that children of school age are all allowed to go to school. Shanker and company perceive schools as instruments to serve, first, the people who work in them, and, second, the children who will do well in them. Children who do poorly in school because of physical or mental handicaps, children who present poor examples, such as pregnant girls, and children who are disruptive—are all perceived as interfering with the rights of others.

That word *disruptive* requires some qualification. I have no quarrel with the suspension from school of a child who fights, shouts, or throws things in class and makes it impossible for the class to proceed. Provided such conduct is proved at a hearing, suspension seems a necessary evil if lesser punishments don't end the disruption. But relatively few children are suspended or expelled from school for actual disruption of class. Far more commonly, they are thrown out of school for conduct outside the classroom, and, most often of all, for truancy. It is the logic of suspensions and expulsion for these causes that I question.

Children alleged to misbehave outside of class should not thereby forfeit their right to an education. Suspension or expulsion for extracurricular conduct, moreover, seems peculiarly irrational. If the purpose of punishment is to prevent such misconduct, does anyone believe it is achieved by depriving a child of the right to attend school? Some children engage in conduct outside of class so serious it violates the criminal law. They should be punished as provided by the laws they violate. Expelling them from school, either as a supplemental or a substitute punishment, is common but wrong.

Truancy is the leading cause of school expulsions. It has a special oddity: The crime and the punishment are identical. Both keep the child out of school.

The belief that schools exist to serve their professional employees and the children who do well in them is best exemplified in the treatment of truants. Instead of trying to get truants to come to school more often, perhaps by making it more attractive to them, the schools exclude them entirely. Ironically, teachers and school administrators often blame vandalism and crime in the vicinity of the school on kids "hanging around" but not actually attending the school. If they did not expel truants, those kids might be in class instead of "hanging around" and getting into mischief.

Joseph and Ernestine Tyson moved into the St. Nicholas Houses, a New York City housing project, in 1954. Mr. Tyson has been ill and has not worked for some time. Ms. Tyson has worked for many years as the housekeeper for a New York City family prominent in public affairs. Her employers speak very highly of Ms. Tyson.

On May 1, 1972, after they had been living in St. Nicholas Houses for eighteen years, the New York City Housing Authority decided the Tysons were "undesirable" tenants. They were ordered evicted. It was not because the Tysons had done anything wrong. They paid their rent on time, kept a clean apartment, and were not noisy. The problem was their son, then twenty-one. He had moved from home two years earlier and thereafter had been arrested and convicted of attempted robbery. He was scheduled for release from prison in August 1973. The Housing Authority didn't want someone with a criminal record moving back into the St. Nicholas Houses to live with his parents or even coming to visit them there. The solution, in the view of the Housing Authority, was to evict the entire family.

At about the time the New York City Housing Authority was ordering the Tysons to move out of the St. Nicholas Houses, it was also trying to build three large apartment houses on the edge of the Forest Hills section of Queens. It was an area of many large apartment buildings, but the three planned by the New York Housing Authority ran into a storm of protest. They would bring poor people and blacks into an upper-middle-class section of the city. In particular, people in Forest Hills objected to the influx of public housing project residents because they said this would create a serious crime problem in their neighborhood.

The housing project in Forest Hills became a major public issue. The controversy over it inflamed the city in a manner reminiscent of the earlier disputes over a civilian review board for the police and community control of the schools. In an effort to win acceptance for the project, the Housing Authority announced its policies for the selection of tenants. A large proportion would be made up of the elderly. Presumably, they would be too feeble to commit crimes against the residents of the surrounding neighborhoods. As for the rest, a careful screening process would keep out anybody with a criminal record.

The project was eventually built on a much smaller scale than originally planned. As promised, part of the project was given over to the elderly. People with criminal records were screened out. In this latter respect, of course, the project was no different from any other New York City Housing Authority project. People with criminal records are always screened out, though it may have been done with more care than usual at Forest Hills.

One lesson of the Forest Hills dispute is that almost no one sees anything wrong with barring people with criminal records from public housing. Most of the supporters of the project welcomed the Housing Authority's announcement about screening tenants. It might mitigate opposition to construction of the project, they hoped. Opponents of the project were not satisfied. They didn't believe all the criminals would be screened out. Hardly anyone suggested it was unfair to deny people with arrest records or conviction records access to public housing. Nor was anyone heard to say that keeping people with criminal records from getting decent housing would probably increase crime, not reduce it.

Public policies denying welfare assistance to intact families, excluding disruptive children from school, and barring public housing to people with criminal records all have a certain logic. They serve the immediate interests of the bureaucracies administering these policies. Welfare administrators can demonstrate that they are not spending the taxpayer's dollar on families with able-bodied males. Schools can point to higher reading scores for their pupils if some children are kept out. Housing administrators can run safer projects if people with criminal records are excluded.

But should these bureaucracies be permitted to pursue policies putting a good gloss on their own performance but, in the process, damaging the public interest? By disrupting families, excluding children from school, and denying homes to people with records of crime, bureaucratically determined public policy has become a cause of crime. These policies greatly exacerbate the problems of transiency and rootlessness at the heart of our crime problem.

Perhaps welfare, housing, and school administrators should be asked to prepare crime-impact evaluations of their own policies. These might resemble the environmental-impact statements required before various federally funded projects can be undertaken. The impact of public policy on crime deserves comparable examination and review because crime is as much a part of our environment as the air we breathe.

The preparation of crime-impact statements could provide a new criterion for measuring bureaucratic performance. A school official could be evaluated according to how large a proportion of the children in the community attend school. This would supplement such criteria as the number of high school graduates going on to college and the reading scores achieved by different grade levels in the schools. An administrator might earn advancement because of his success in attracting truants back to classes rather than for his skill at severing all their ties to school.

If the idea of crime-impact statements were to catch on, the important thing would be to insist that evaluations attempt to measure the impact on society at large and not just on the institution itself. A board of education might be able to demonstrate that its own schools would be safer if some children were excluded. But the test should be whether the entire community would be safer. Public policy is poorly served when little islands of safety are created and all the space in between is too dangerous to navigate. The institutions serving us must be required to look out for our well-being, not just their own.

PART TWO
Punishment

11
Recommended:
A Double Standard

"A kangaroo court" was one of the ways the defendant described the proceedings when given the right to address the court just before his sentencing. "I listened without interrupting," the judge told a colleague over cocktails. "Finally, when he was through, I simply gave the son of a bitch five years instead of the four" earlier intended.

This story is told about an unidentified fellow judge by Federal Judge Marvin Frankel, one of the country's most respected jurists. Frankel has been trying to awaken his fellow judges to the lawlessness of their sentencing practices. Writing about the extra year behind bars for the "kangaroo court" remarks, Frankel asks: "Would we tolerate an act of Congress penalizing such an outburst by a year in prison? The question, however rhetorical, misses one truly exquisite note of agony: that the wretch sentenced by Judge X never knew, because he was never told, how the fifth year of his term came to be added." [1]

Robert François Damiens probably understood the reasons for the punishment he received. He had committed as heinous a crime as the judges could imagine, and they wanted retribution, pure and simple. Damiens had attempted to murder King Louis XV, and indeed had succeeded in stabbing the monarch, drawing a little royal blood.

131

Excruciating tortures were devised for Damiens. His legs were placed in iron "boots," and at fifteen-minute intervals wedges were inserted and tightened. Damiens screamed, but there was much worse to come. His hands were dipped in flaming sulfur, various parts of his body were pinched by red-hot tongs, molten lead and boiling oil were poured on the open wounds, and finally, to the delight of a crowd gathered in front of the Hôtel de Ville in Paris, Damiens was torn limb from limb by four giant horses whipped to a frenzy by his executioners. He remained alive until nothing but a bleeding torso was left.

In 1764, seven years after the torture-killing of Damiens, a little book by a young Italian reformer offered the Age of Enlightenment's first systematic thinking on punishment. *Essay on Crimes and Punishments,* by Cesare Beccaria, was a denunciation of the cruelty of his age. Beccaria was far ahead of his own time, and perhaps even of our time. "Capital punishment," Beccaria wrote, "cannot be useful because of the example of barbarity it presents. . . . To me it seems an absurdity that the laws, which are the expression of the public will, which abhor and which punish murder, should themselves commit one; and that, to deter citizens from private assassinations, they should themselves order a public murder." Today, more than two centuries later, most of our state legislatures and the United States Congress are busy passing new laws reaffirming their belief in the death penalty.

Beccaria had great influence in the American Colonies. The young John Adams invoked him in his opening statement to the jury in defense of the British soldiers on trial for the "Boston Massacre." "May it please your honors, and you gentlemen of the jury," said Adams, "I am for the prisoners at the bar, and shall apologize for it only in the words of the Marquis Beccaria: If I can but be the instrument of preserving one life, his blessing and tears of transport shall be a sufficient consolation to me for the contempt of all mankind." (Adams's skilled advocacy saved several lives, and the British soldiers escaped with only brands on their thumbs for firing on a crowd of Boston citizens.)

Thomas Jefferson, too, was an admirer of Beccaria and believed with the Italian reformer that to deter crime, punishments need not be severe, but they should be sure. "The principle of Beccaria is sound," said Jefferson in an article for an encyclopedia. "Let the legislators be merciful, but the executors of the law inexorable."

The prohibition of "cruel and unusual punishment" in the United States Constitution is an enduring testament to Beccaria's influence on the Founding Fathers. He thought such punishments needless and believed they set a savage example that could only produce further crime and bloodshed. Prison, he thought, was the proper alternative to execution and torture.

"The object of punishment," said Beccaria, "is simply to prevent the criminal from injuring anew his fellow citizens [today, we call this 'incapacitation' of the criminal] and to deter others [we call this 'general deterrence'] from committing similar injuries." Both incapacitation and general deterrence are justifications for punishment in contemporary American sentencing practices. But it is rarely possible to tell in what degree one or another of these criteria inspired a particular punishment. They have been hopelessly intertwined with each other and with several other rationales for punishment. That is why the wretch in Judge Frankel's story suffered the "exquisite agony" of never knowing why he spent the fifth year—or any of the previous four years—in prison.

Foremost among today's criteria for sentencing is one that had not occurred to Beccaria, rehabilitation. As Ramsey Clark insists, "Rehabilitation must be the goal of modern corrections. Every other consideration should be subordinated to it." [2] The prevailing view of enlightened people is that if only prisoners were treated properly, their criminal tendencies could be curbed. The renowned psychiatrist Dr. Karl Menninger asks:

Do I believe there is effective treatment for offenders, and that they *can* be changed? *Most certainly and definitively I do.* Not all cases, to be sure; there are also some physical afflictions which we cannot cure at the moment. Some provision has to be made for incurables—pending new knowledge—and these will include some offenders. But I believe the majority of them would prove to be curable. The willfulness and the viciousness of offenders are part of the thing for which they have to be treated. These must not thwart the therapeutic attitude.[3]

The rehabilitation ideal is a legacy of a period more than a half century after publication of Beccaria's *Essay on Crimes and Punishments*. Americans in the 1820s and 1830s discarded some of the Calvinist insistence on the innate evil of humankind. Instead, reformers of the period contended that crime and other forms of deviancy were a product of a corrupt environment. The cure was to remove the criminal from the setting that had made him go wrong. In the sanitized environment of a prison, with an orderly regimen, the Jacksonian era optimists believed the criminal would be rehabilitated.

Before the nineteenth century, prisons usually served a function similar to the jails we have today. They incarcerated people not yet tried. After trial, the lucky prisoner whose innocence was vindicated would go free. If he was found guilty, he would be branded, flogged, maimed, executed, or even tortured to death like Damiens.

The prisons of the Jacksonian period were built far from the cities. Communication with relatives and friends of the prisoner outside was made as difficult as possible. That way, so the theory went, the inmate would be more effectively separated from those influences that had led him astray. In prison, isolation, steady work, and steady habits would bring great changes in the person. A boundless faith in the capacity of prisons to rehabilitate is epitomized in the words of a nineteenth-century prison chaplain, James B. F. Finley: "Could we all be put on prison fare, for the space of two or three generations, the world would ultimately be the better for it. Indeed, should society change places with the prisoners, so far as habits are concerned, taking to itself the regularity, and temperance, and sobriety of a good prison," we would all be better off. "As it is, taking this world and the next together," said Finley, "the prisoner has the advantage." [4]

Other countries learned from the new American Republic. Distinguished Europeans such as Alexis de Tocqueville and Gustave de Beaumont visited the United States to spread the good news about these prisons that rehabilitated their inmates. Later generations in Europe and the United States maintained their faith in rehabilitation long after it should have become evident it wasn't taking place. Liberals on both sides of the Atlantic are fond of quoting a pre–World War I speech by Winston Churchill to the British House of Commons. "The mood and temper of the public with regard to the treatment of crime and criminals is one of the most unfailing tests of the civilization of any country," said Churchill. He called for "a desire and eagerness to rehabilitate in the world of industry ... tireless efforts toward the discovery of curative and regenerative processes." The physical isolation and impenetrability of prisons—part of what was supposed to work such great changes on inmates—was principally effective in making it difficult to examine the institutions critically. Besides, there was always an explanation of failure. The fault was with the way a particular prison was administered. It could be cured—and the prisoners could be cured—by some reforms.

The failure of prisons to rehabilitate prisoners parallels the failure of mental hospitals to cure mental patients, or of juvenile reformatories to reform juveniles. These other big institutions are a legacy of the same faith that created prisons, and they have been as bitterly disappointing. All in all, coerced "treatment" of social deviancy doesn't seem to work. "In the end," said the McKay Commission, which investigated the 1971 uprising at New York State's Attica prison, "the promise of rehabilitation had become a cruel joke."

A few isolated success stories are reported in the scholarly literature. But as David Rothman has noted, "We must be especially wary of 'model' programs. There is not sufficient cause to assume that all such programs will be effective and decent simply because one charismatic personality manages to effect some good." [5]

Nor should we be seduced by the occasional extraordinary prisoner who credits incarceration with his own rehabilitation. "In the hectic pace of the world today," the late Malcolm X wrote in his autobiography, "there is no time for meditation, or for deep thought. A prisoner has time that he can put to good use. I'd put prison second to college as the best place for a man to go if he needs to do some thinking. If he's motivated, in prison he can change his life." [6]

The Quakers, who played such a large part in the prison movement of the first half of the nineteenth century, and who bequeathed us the word *penitentiary* to describe institutions where a convicted criminal was expected to be penitent, would have rejoiced to hear the words of Malcolm X. He was the fulfillment of their hopes for prisons. But governments are incapable of systematically duplicating the Malcolm X experience. As he said, a prisoner has to be "motivated" if prison is to "change his life." What is there that prison administrators can do to foster such motivation?

Malcolm X was not the only prisoner whose rehabilitation in prison appears to have grown out of an association with the Black Muslim movement, which first developed behind bars. But that movement was hardly a creature of prison administrations. It was a revolt against prison administrations. As the McKay Commission said, "If anyone was rehabilitated, it was in spite of Attica, not because of it." The thinking, reading, letter writing, and organizing that created groups such as the Black Muslims may be the best "rehabilitation" that can take place in prison. Yet one can hardly justify a theory of punishment based on the hope that some people will rebel against prison conditions. Nor can one count on the emergence of constructive rebellions.

No one has yet been able to identify a model of incarceration that if put to general use would rehabilitate criminals any better than simply leaving them alone. There is an extensive literature on the subject. Hundreds of studies have been done. Robert Martinson, now chairman of the Department of Sociology at the City University of New York, spent six years on the staff of the New York State Governor's Special Committee on Criminal Offenders, surveying what was known about rehabilitation. The committee had been organized to show how prisons rehabilitated their inmates. More and better rehabilitation programs, it was intended to prove, should be incorporated in New York State's prison system. Despite the desire to come up with something that worked, nothing could be found.

I am bound to say [Martinson has written about his research] that these data, involving over two hundred studies and hundreds of thousands of individuals as they do, are the best available and give us very little reason to hope that we have in fact found a sure way of reducing recidivism through rehabilitation. This is not to say we found no instances of success or partial success; it is only to say these instances have been isolated, producing no clear pattern to indicate the efficacy of any particular method of treatment.[7]

A similarly dispiriting conclusion about rehabilitation emerged from a previous review of the published literature. Walter C. Bailey examined a hundred studies on treatment. Many of them claimed success. Bailey found almost no reliable evidence to support the claims of effectiveness.[8] That goes for big prisons and small prisons; for maximum-security and minimum-security prisons; for prisons with more or less regimentation, psychiatric treatment, behavior modification, street supervision, vocational training, literacy training, and whatever else might be imagined.

Efforts to rehabilitate people are, no doubt, rooted in humanitarian values. But many people find it more repugnant to be in prison for their own good than for some less exalted motives. C. S. Lewis has written:

To be taken without consent from my home and friends; to lose my liberty; to undergo all those assaults on my personality which modern psychotherapy knows how to deliver; to be re-made after some pattern of "normality" hatched in a Viennese laboratory to which I never professed allegiance; to know that this process will never end until either my captors have succeeded or I have grown wise enough to cheat them with apparent success—who cares whether this is called Punishment or not? [9]

Lewis, a British philosopher, theologian, and also the author of widely popular books for children, rightly identifies the notion of the indeterminate sentence as a product of the rehabilitation ideal. After all, if one believes in rehabilitating people, it makes sense to hold them until someone determines they have been cured. Yet it is hard to imagine anything more hateful to prisoners than the indeterminate sentence, even if it is a logical consequence of the desire to help them.

Despite its demonstrated failure, the idea that people can be rehabilitated while locked up continues to beguile reformers. In its latest incarnation, rehabilitation is called "behavior modification." If isolation, prayer, and steady habits won't reform prisoners, the up-to-date behavior modifiers want to try out "aversive conditioning." As photographs of naked children are flashed on a screen, child molesters watching the pictures get very painful electric shocks in their genitals. These alternate with photographs of naked adult women minus the electric shocks.[10]

Some behavior-modification programs are more subtle. No electric shocks. Instead, inmates are deprived of the few amenities of prison life—variety in diet, visitors, showers, mail, literature, and exercise. As they conform to a desirable pattern of behavior, the amenities are restored. Desirable behavior turns out to be not complaining and not agitating other prisoners. All this may make prisoners a lot more docile for prison-management purposes. But if it works, it probably deprives prisoners of the initiative to better themselves once out of prison.

Prison did make Malcolm X modify his behavior, but not because it stripped him of motivation. He brought to the prison intense motivation and found in prison the opportunity he had never had before to make himself over. In prison, Malcolm X read widely—Will Durant, H. G. Wells, W. E. B. DuBois, Harriet Beecher Stowe—corresponded with Elijah Muhammad, and agitated other prisoners. Behavior-modification programs, as we know them, would have discouraged or prohibited all these things. A behavior-modification program of the sort now in vogue could well have prevented Malcolm X from rehabilitating himself.

Rehabilitation of self, unorganized and perhaps anarchic, is the best we can expect in prisons. I doubt it could possibly happen as often as if convicted criminals were left alone outside prisons. Not that great numbers of criminals naturally and quickly rehabilitate themselves outside prison—only that it seems to happen even less frequently inside.

At its worst, what goes under the name of "behavior modification" is just a streamlined version of the punishment meted out to Damiens. At its best, it is probably ineffectual. Even so, its advent breathes new life into the myth that people are put behind bars for their own good.

The failure of planned and organized rehabilitation doesn't mean prisons serve no purpose. Convicts are not all as saintly as Victor Hugo's Jean Valjean. Some of them deserve to be in prison, but for our good and not for their own good. It is folly to expect any significant numbers of prisoners to come out better or less dangerous than they went in.

With this exception. Prisoners are older when they get out than when they went in. And age makes a big difference. The propensity to commit crimes declines precipitously with maturity. Whether the criminal ages inside a prison cell or at liberty, after the passage of years he is less dangerous. Which brings us back to Beccaria.

"To prevent the criminal from injuring anew," or to incapacitate him, was one of the objects of punishment of Beccaria. This surely takes place while a person is in prison. And if he is kept in prison until age thirty or thirty-five or forty, chances are that most of his propensity to crime will be behind him.

Here is what the FBI crime reports for 1973 show about the decline in criminality by age. Aggregating the figures for crimes included in the FBI's crime index—murder, manslaughter, rape, robbery, aggravated assault, burglary, larceny, and auto theft—84 percent of all arrests involve people twenty-nine or younger.

Persons thirty-four or younger account for 89.1 percent of all arrests for these crimes, and persons thirty-nine or younger account for 92.4 percent of such arrests. The criminal tendency has apparently burned out of most people by age thirty and out of almost everybody by age thirty-five or forty.

By holding people in prison until they are in their thirties, then, some people *are* rehabilitated. But not by prisons. They are rehabilitated by getting older.

Is it fair to hold people in prison to incapacitate them until they have outgrown crime? In the case of a very few criminals, I believe the answer is yes.

Some people who have committed very serious crimes of violence should be given incapacitating sentences to protect everyone else. The crimes I have in mind are murder, forcible rape, robbery, aggravated assault, and arson. But, certainly, not everyone who commits these crimes. Only in those cases where the nature and circumstances of the crime committed or the person's previous history of violent crime makes it plain that society cannot afford to take a chance on letting the criminal go free during the years most serious crime takes place.

Incapacitation as a justification for sentencing is under serious attack. It has been sharply questioned by the Committee on the Study of Incarceration, a group of outstanding lawyers, historians, sociologists, and psychologists assembled by the Field Foundation to rethink the theory and practice of sentencing. The committee notes the fallibility of efforts to predict who will engage in violent crime. Therefore, the committee says, to ensure that people who will engage in violence are confined in prison, a great many other people will also have to be confined. It is unjust, in this view, to confine the nondangerous in order to be sure of incapacitating the dangerous. The committee also questions "whether it is just to punish someone more severely on account of what he is expected to do in the future, even if the prediction were accurate." [11]

Norval Morris, dean of the School of Law at the University of Chicago, also argues against predictive restraint. It "must be rejected," he says, "because it presupposes a capacity to predict quite beyond our present or foreseeable technical ability." [12] Moreover, Morris observes, the pressure to overpredict would be overwhelming.

If one is unsure about the likely future violent behavior of a person currently under control and for whom that control can legally be prolonged, the benefit of the doubt had better be given to any future possible victim rather than to the criminal or to the prisoner. What is wonderfully convenient about this over-prediction of risk is that the predictor does not know who in particular, as a person, as eyes to be met, he is needlessly holding. Further, he is most unlikely to precipitate any political or administrative trouble as a result of ordering imprisonment or prolonging its duration. By contrast, one is quite likely to be in water too warm for comfort when those people whom one has released, but who could legally have been detained, *do* involve themselves in crimes of violence, particularly if those crimes are sensationally reported. Hence the path of administrative and political safety is the path of over-predicted risk. [13]

Some people, the members of the Committee on the Study of Incarceration and Professor Morris not among them, believe the problem of prediction could be solved by giving it over to psychiatrists instead of judges. For anyone who clings to the hope that psychiatrists are possessed of greater prophetic powers than other people, I recommend an article by my colleagues in the ACLU, Bruce J. Ennis and Thomas R. Litwack. Its title, "Psychiatry and the Presumption of Expertise: Flipping Coins in the Courtroom," is a capsule statement of the evidence the authors have collected. The article persuasively demonstrates what most members of the profession readily acknowledge: Psychiatrists cannot predict violence.

Human behavior is difficult to understand [Ennis and Litwack conclude], and, at present, impossible to predict. Subject to constitutional limitations, the decision to deprive another human of liberty is not a psychiatric judgment but a social judgment. We shall have to decide how much we value individual freedom; how much we care about privacy and self-determination; how much deviance we can tolerate—or how much suffering. There are no "experts" to make those decisions for us.[14]

While I share the skepticism of Messrs. Morris, Ennis, and Litwack about the utility of psychiatric predictions, some of the evidence they adduce in support of their arguments could be read just as persuasively as an argument for incapacitating sentences. These opponents of predictive restraint find an important lesson in the consequences of a 1966 Supreme Court decision, *Baxstrom* v. *Herold*. The case involved 969 persons held after their prison terms expired in the maximum-security institutions of Dannemora and Mattewan in New York State. Their confinement was continued because psychiatrists said they were mentally ill and too dangerous for release. The Supreme Court said the 969 could not constitutionally be held longer than their original prison terms without the usual procedures required by law for committing people to mental hospitals. As a result, all 969 were immediately transferred to civil mental hospitals.

Despite the psychiatrists' predictions that these were all dangerous people, a follow-up study showed they caused no great harm following their release from Dannemora and Mattewan. Within a year, 147 were discharged to the community. Only 7 proved so troublesome as to be recommitted to hospitals for the criminal insane. Four years later, 27 percent of the *Baxstrom* patients were living in the community, and only 3 percent were in prison or hospitals for the criminal insane. There were only 9 criminal convictions among them, and only 2 for felonies.

Impressive as the consequences of the *Baxstrom* decision are for making Professor Morris's case against predictive restraint and the Ennis-Litwack case against psychiatric prophecy, they can also be seen as confirming nothing more than the observation that dangerousness diminishes with age. By the time of the *Baxstrom* decision, the 969 had been in Dannemora and Mattewan an average of thirteen years. Moreover, they first entered these institutions after completing prison sentences. They had been behind bars for very long periods. Even if the psychiatric judgments of dangerousness were accurate when first made—and I am as skeptical of this as anyone—they were no longer valid by 1966 when the Supreme Court decided the patients must be released from institutions for the criminal insane. From what little we know of human behavior, aging is the surest method of reducing dangerousness short of execution or maiming. The sharp decline of dangerousness with age is one of the principal arguments in favor of incapacitating sentences. It allows us to consider such sentences for persons who commit certain crimes of violence without resort to abhorrently long sentences such as life in prison, or twenty-five or thirty years. For purposes of incapacitation such prolonged sentences are superfluous.

Anyone proposing to put a human being in a cage for ten or fifteen years must bear a very heavy burden. Only extremely serious crimes of violence could possibly justify such drastic punishment. I have in mind murder, rape, arson with intent to kill, or aggravated assault with intent to kill. Most important, I would require that such a serious crime of violence be a "public crime" if it is to yield an incapacitating sentence. Lesser "public crimes" of robbery and aggravated assault (absent intent to kill) could also result in an incapacitating sentence in my scheme if the criminal had previously been convicted of a crime of violence.

I define a "public crime" of violence as an assault on a stranger or as a crime performed for profit or committed by a person previously convicted of a violent crime.

The great majority of murders and most other very serious crimes of violence are not "public crimes." They are products of tangled personal relationships and can be described as "private crimes." While the damage to a particular victim of either kind of crime may be equal, "private crime" does not terrorize society at large. It does not tear at the very fabric of social order. Most of us can arrange our lives to avoid private crimes of violence. Public crime, on the other hand, is random. We do not know when we will be struck from behind as we take a walk, or be raped, or be shot down as we sip a beer in the neighborhood tavern that happens to be the target of a trigger-happy holdup man.

As our laws are written today, they do not distinguish

between private crime and public crime. Take rape. "A male is guilty of rape in the first degree," in the words of the typical rape statute, "when he engages in sexual intercourse with a female by forcible compulsion." That is all it says. Then consider the following two cases of rape. They happened to take place in the same week and in the same city.

In the first case, both man and woman were in the armed forces. She appeared to regard her sexual adventures lightly and had boasted of the number of men on the base she had engaged sexually. He had known her for some time, though this was the first time they had spent time alone. They had been together all day, mostly on the beach, and had engaged in extensive sexual foreplay. In the evening they went to his apartment. At the beach they had been drinking beer, and in the apartment each had a Scotch. For reasons that are not clear, they got into an argument. It culminated in rape. Along the way, he showed her the gun he kept in a night-table drawer and threatened to use it.

The second case involves a young divorced woman living with her daughter, age two, and her son, age four. She was preparing their dinner in the kitchen when she heard a noise in the living room. A man had entered through an unlocked door. He had a knife. If she didn't submit, he would use it on the children. They were shut in the bedroom; he raped their mother, cut the telephone line, and left.

As the law now stands, both rapists face the same penalties. Both women were raped. In one case, the rapist had a gun, in the other a knife. The soldier with the gun might have gotten a longer sentence than the rapist with the knife who had threatened to hurt the children. I don't think the sentences should be the same or that there should be any possibility of a longer sentence for the soldier-rapist.

It may be just as awful for the woman soldier to have been raped as for any other woman. If sentences are to be based entirely on the injury to the victim, rapists should all be treated alike. But other women don't have a great deal to fear from the woman soldier's rapist. They can avoid the circumstances of that rape. But almost any woman is vulnerable to the rapist who suddenly appears in her living room or attacks her in a hallway or on a dark street. Rapists like that menace the lives of many women who avoid risky personal relationships.

Or take murder.

One man calls a police precinct to lure a policeman to a deserted building. As the policeman enters on what he thinks is a mission to help someone, the man who made the phone call guns him down.

In another case, a narcotics addict is scheduled to testify against three undercover narcotics detectives accused of shaking down dealers and themselves peddling heroin. The day before he is scheduled to testify, the witness is found bound, gagged, and shot in the head.

In another case, a man and his young son go on a spree of robbery and rape in suburban communities. While the father molests the victims, the son ransacks the homes. A nurse refuses to submit to rape, and the father murders her.

Contrast these murders with the more everyday variety: the barroom fights between old acquaintances, the lovers' quarrels ending in death, the family arguments settled with gunfire. The FBI reports that, nationally, 78 percent of all murders are of this sort. In each case, the victim is dead. But consider the societal terror inflicted by the man who ambushed the policeman, the contract murderer of the court witness, and the sex-and-robbery murderer who took his young son along. The circumstances of some murders, though not most, justify a society in refusing to take a chance on the murderers during the violent years of their youth. Those people deserve incapacitating sentences.

And what of the rape or murder that is the culmination of an argument between two people with a previous relationship to each other? Assume, also, that the murderer or rapist has never previously been convicted of a crime of violence. What punishment should be meted out to such a criminal?

For such a crime of violence, I advocate a maximum permissible sentence of three years in prison. The purpose would not be to incapacitate the criminal. If he was dangerous when he went in, the elapsed time would not significantly mitigate the danger by the time he got out. Nor would the purpose be to rehabilitate the criminal. *Not* incarcerating a criminal, I believe, is more likely to produce rehabilitation than putting him in prison. The purpose would be to stop other people from committing similar crimes because, if they did, they, too, would go to prison. In short, the purpose is general deterrence.[15]

Property crimes, I believe, should incur still shorter sentences—I propose a maximum punishment of one year in prison. This would be the penalty for a nighttime burglar of a private residence who has previously been convicted of a similar crime. Unlike robbery, this crime does not directly threaten violence. It is the most serious of all property crimes, however, because there is a significant *potential* for violence if the homeowner or apartment dweller surprises the burglar in the act. Other property crimes—larceny, burglary of a place of business, etc.—would get lesser punishments. First offenders convicted of lesser property crimes would get warnings. The next most serious form of punishment would be nighttime or weekend confinement—allowing the criminal to keep a job or get a job during the daytime. Continuous confinement for periods of ten days, twenty days, or thirty days, and so on up to one year, would be considered major punishments. They would be given out only sparingly as the seriousness of the offense warranted.

It will be objected that these punishments are too light. I disagree. Let the reader contemplate spending the next four weekends in jail or going to jail after work every night for a month. If we could only put out of mind the outsized punishments we read about in the daily press, we would comprehend the severity of the punishments I propose, and they could serve as deterrents.

Moreover, there are things the state can do for the victims of property crime. Within reason, the victims should be compensated for their losses. While there is little or nothing the state can do to compensate the woman who has been raped or the murder victim, property-crime victims can be helped with cash compensations. I would rather see the state spend money to aid victims than spend $10,000 to $15,000 a year to keep a burglar in jail. That is especially true when one considers that the three-to-five-year prison sentences so commonly given to perpetrators of property crime may be no greater deterrents than the shorter sentences I propose. While a three-to-five-year sentence isn't long enough to incapacitate a burglar until he burns out, it is long enough to disrupt the criminal's ties to family, friends, work, and community. When he leaves prison, the prisoner without ties is more likely than ever to turn to crime as a career.

There are many objections to a reliance on general deterrence as a justification for imprisonment. Some are very troubling, and while I urge reliance on a deterrence theory, I do it with a certain diffidence. To explain how I would use general deterrence and why I rely upon it, I will list what seem to me the most serious objections to it.

First objection: Much of what we know about crime suggests that certain crimes are more easily deterred than others by increasing the severity of punishment. Suppose, for example, the penalty for jaywalking were escalated to a minimum of one year in prison and the law were systematically enforced. Jaywalking would be eliminated. Similarly, one might readily deter tax evasion by establishing severe penalties and rigorously prosecuting violators. Other more serious crimes—family-argument murders, many sex crimes—are not so easily deterrable. In ancient Rome, the punishment for a parricide was to be stripped naked, whipped, and then sewn into a sack crammed with a dog, a rooster, a monkey, and a snake. The entire bundle was then thrown into the Tiber River to drown the person who had murdered his father. (Presumably, the animals also drowned.) Despite the cruelty of this punishment, we learn from reading Cicero's defenses of Romans charged with murder that the crime of parricide seems to have been fairly common. The severity of the punishment apparently was not a very effective deterrent to a crime such as parricide. Does this mean society should establish more severe penalties for jaywalking or tax evasion than for less deterrable crimes such as murder or rape?

Response: No. Deterrence must be limited by proportionality. It is unjust to punish a person more severely because the crime he has committed is more deterrable. If deterrence were the only value served by a criminal justice system, it might make sense to punish a less serious crime more severely than a grave crime. A system of criminal justice must also be fair. And, in fairness, more serious punishments must be reserved for more serious crimes.

Second objection: Wouldn't deterrence be served best by imposing exemplary penalties on more conspicuous individuals or more conspicuous crimes? Anthony Lewis, writing in *The New York Times* after Judge John Sirica imposed two-and-one-half-to-eight-year prison terms on H. R. Haldeman, John Mitchell, and John Ehrlichman, pointed out that the sentences were "severe for a first offense, a white collar crime." But these sentences were proper, Lewis argued, because "the crime has a special character when it involves the corruption of the highest power in the country.... The justification of these sentences has to lie in deterrence." [16] In a variation on this theme, Norval Morris has noted that

Not every tax felon need be imprisoned, only a number sufficient to keep the law's promises and to encourage the rest of us to honesty in our tax returns. The present arrangements for imprisoning federal tax offenders are an object lesson in the parsimonious application of general deterrent sanctions: approximately 80 million tax returns were filed in 1972; only 43 percent of the 825 individuals convicted for tax fraud were jailed.[17]

Does reliance on general deterrence mean the likes of Haldeman, Mitchell, and Ehrlichman should be treated more severely by the criminal law because of their high rank? Does it mean a few tax evaders should be selected at random for harsh treatment so we can make examples of them?

Response: No. Again, I would reject any scheme of deterrence that is unfair. Haldeman, Mitchell, and Ehrlichman should have been punished no more severely (and no more lightly) than anyone else. The only limit on the *number* of tax evaders punished should be derived from the shortage of tax enforcement personnel.

I am against exemplary treatment of conspicuous persons because it is unfair. In addition, I am skeptical of the deterrent value of such a system. Deterrence, I believe, works if the law follows Beccaria's theory: Punishment need not be cruel, but it should be sure. A recent examination of scholarly literature on deterrence by Gordon Tullock, an economist, appears to support Beccaria's theory.

Tullock says he has been unable to discover any "efforts to test the deterrent effect of punishment scientifically until about 1950." Since then, the effectiveness of deterrence has been studied by both economists and sociologists. In general, the economists embarked on their studies expecting to find that deterrence worked. The sociologists started expecting to find it did not work. They "took out their statistical tools," Tullock reports, "with the intent of confirming what was then the conventional wisdom of their field—that crime cannot be deterred by punishment . . . they found out they were wrong." Most of the sociologists and a good many of the economists also tried to determine whether the severity of the punishment or the likelihood of it had the greater deterrent impact. "More often than not," says Tullock, "the researchers have found that the frequency with which the punishment is applied is of greater importance than its severity." [18]

Third objection: If research demonstrates that increasing the maximum sentence for a crime from a year in prison to six years in prison greatly increases deterrence, wouldn't reliance on a theory of deterrence require a consequent increase in the penalties?

Response: No. Again, fairness must be a constraint on deterrence. Regardless of the findings of research, it is wrong to escalate penalties beyond what is just in response to a particular crime.

Moreover, I very much doubt the validity of any such research. In a society that treats twenty- and twenty-five-year sentences as routine, the significance of such extraordinarily long time periods is depreciated. With a more sensible system of sentencing, the much shorter sentences I propose would no longer *appear* so light. Three years in prison is a very, very long period of time behind bars. The reader need only think back to what he or she was doing three years ago. Think of the intervening events. Then think of spending all that time in prison. Try the same thing with one year, or six months, or even a month. We have cheapened the currency of punishment by inflating prison sentences. Moreover, the problem has been greatly exacerbated by everybody's realization that a twenty-year sentence is not really a twenty-year sentence. There will be time off for good behavior, we tell ourselves, and parole boards will much further reduce the actual time behind bars. A person with a twenty-year sentence may be out of prison in five years (or he may not), making fifteen years of his life of no more significance than something to depend on "good behavior" and the hurriedly and casually formed opinion of a parole board.

Fourth objection: If general deterrence is a justification for punishment, why is it even necessary for the person we punish to have committed a crime? "All the purposes of deterrence will be equally served by the punishment of an innocent victim," C. S. Lewis has written, "provided that the public can be cheated into thinking him guilty." [19]

Response: Still again, I rely upon fairness as a limitation upon deterrence. The unfairness of punishing an innocent man to deter others is so manifest as not to require further discussion.

In each of these responses, I have qualified my adherence to deterrence by insisting it must be limited by fairness. Sentences may not be increased or imposed on conspicuous persons or innocent persons even if to do so would make their deterrent value more effective. Why, then, adhere to deterrence? Why not join the Committee on the Study of Incarceration and others who believe that "commensurate deserts" or "retribution" are the proper grounds for punishing people who commit crimes?

Deterrence is part of the criminal law's very purpose.[20] By enumerating certain kinds of conduct that will be punished, the criminal law aims to prevent us from committing those acts. And by establishing a scale of punishments, the criminal law advises us of the extent of the injury to others caused by certain kinds of conduct.

Reliance on commensurate deserts alone is tautological—a punishment is just because it is just. Moreover, there are grave difficulties flowing from exclusive reliance on commensurate deserts to justify punishment.

Advocates of commensurate deserts as the exclusive basis for punishment are principally concerned with the injury done to the victim of crime. One woman who has been raped has been injured as gravely as another. A murder victim is equally dead whether the killer was a friend who was drinking or a robber who stuck up a grocery store and killed the occupants to be sure there were no witnesses. The public crime–private crime distinction I make is immaterial if punishment is to be entirely a matter of commensurate deserts. Several criteria have been traditionally invoked to vary the length of sentences. They include the degree of provocation, whether the criminal committed previous crimes, whether the criminal makes a career of crime, whether the criminal profited from the crime, and whether the crime was particularly brutal. Except for brutality, none of these should carry weight to a judge entirely motivated by a theory of commensurate deserts. The rest look to the criminal rather than the crime. And it is critical to the theory of commensurate deserts that the punishment must fit the crime, not the criminal.[21]

Unless it is extraordinarily harsh to people who commit what I have labeled private crimes, a scheme of punishment based on commensurate deserts, by itself, could allow the criminal I believe to merit an incapacitating sentence to be out of prison after a relatively short period. But that would probably lead to great public protest. Almost no one would be willing to let Juan Corona, James Earl Ray, Charles Manson, Richard Speck, or Sirhan Sirhan out of prison at any early date. Yet inevitably there are some people of this sort in the criminal justice system. Their presence seems to ensure that a sentencing system entirely built on commensurate deserts will be too severe by far. The victims of these killers are no more dead than the victims of any other killers. To diminish the distorting impact these criminals have on the entire system, we need a sentencing rationale for treating them very differently from friends and relatives who kill each other in the course of heated arguments. The public crime–private crime approach, resulting in a dual system of punishment comprising incapacitation and deterrence (both to be limited by fairness), seems to make sense in theory and to be useful in practice.

12

Plea Bargaining: The Need for Reform

Lee Earl Johnson, a forty-three-year-old truck driver, was in a lot of trouble. He was drunk. The stolen Ford Thunderbird he was riding in had just crashed into a Cadillac limousine with eleven occupants. Two were killed instantly. Seven other passengers in the limousine were seriously injured.

Johnson was charged with two counts of murder and ten other felonies. Bail was set at $75,000, an amount intended to keep Johnson in jail while his fate was being settled. He stayed in jail for fourteen months while his lawyer bargained for a plea with the New York County assistant district attorney assigned to the case. The DA offered eighteen to twenty years in prison, but Johnson refused. Then something remarkable happened. In what a judge later described as "an almost cursory, off-the-cuff, indolent manner," another assistant district attorney told Johnson's lawyer there were two witnesses who said Johnson was innocent.

The witnesses were both college students. They had watched the Thunderbird speeding down New York's Lexington Avenue at 1:30 A.M. on December 23, 1973, and crash into the limousine at Eightieth Street.

Immediately after impact [New York Supreme Court Justice Peter McQuillan subsequently wrote in his opinion in the case], each student

153

observed a man open the driver's door of the Ford from the interior, exit from the vehicle and then run west on 80th Street. They heard the police shouting for someone to stop this man. They saw the injured defendant [Johnson] seated on the passenger side of the Ford. They testified that he appeared to be drunk when removed from the vehicle on the passenger side.

On the following day, Monday, the students read press accounts of the tragedy. It was reported that multiple charges were lodged against the defendant. They were concerned that perhaps the wrong man was being held responsible for the crime. . . . On Tuesday, December 25, the students went to the *Daily News*. There, a city editor referred them to a police station where they were interviewed by a detective. On Thursday, they were notified by telephone to come the next day to the district attorney's office. On Friday, December 28, they were interviewed by an assistant district attorney. The case was presented to a grand jury on January 11, 16 and 25.

At the December 28 meeting in the district attorney's office, one of the students asked the prosecutor, when she first met him, "if he was Johnson's attorney and he told me, no, he was the assistant district attorney and he was handling the case. I asked him if he had an attorney and would I be contacted, and he said, yes, you would be contacted if it is necessary and nothing was said about Johnson having an attorney." Both students testified before the grand jury on January 11.

Along the way, Johnson's attorney had made a routine request for information about any "exculpatory" material. Even though the law requires this sort of information to be made available to defense counsel, the New York County District Attorney's Office, reputedly the best in the country, simply did not respond to the request. That was not unusual. It typifies the slipshod procedure by which courts, prosecutors, and defense attorneys deal with great chunks of people's lives.

The procedure is known as plea bargaining. Without it, we are told, the courts would break down. There just isn't enough time to give trials to all the people accused of crime.

Sometimes plea bargaining injures the innocent, such as Lee Earl Johnson. Sometimes it lessens the punishment of the guilty.

Charles Yukl's bargained plea got him out of prison after only five years. It was not a very long term behind bars, considering his crime. He had committed an especially brutal sex murder. The victim was a young woman who studied music under Yukl's tutelage.

One reason Yukl may have gotten such a favorable plea was his choice of defense counsel. Yukl was represented by a former police commissioner of the City of New York, a man with many good friends in the District Attorney's Office.

Shortly after getting out of prison, Yukl advertised in a show-business publication for aspiring young actresses. A young woman answered the advertisement. She was found sometime later in Yukl's apartment building, murdered in exactly the same brutal fashion as the music student five years earlier.

There is nothing very new about plea bargaining. "If all the defendants should combine to refuse to plead guilty, and should dare to hold out," Justice Henry T. Lummus of the Supreme Judicial Court of Massachusetts pointed out forty years ago,

they could break down the administration of criminal justice in any state in the Union. But they dare not hold out, for such as were tried and convicted could hope for no leniency. The prosecutor is like a man armed with a revolver who is cornered by a mob. A concerted rush would overwhelm him, but each individual in the mob fears that he might be one of those shot during the rush. When defendants plead guilty, they expect more leniency than when convicted by a jury, and must receive it, or there will be no such pleas. The truth is, that a criminal court can operate only by inducing the great mass of actually guilty defendants to plead guilty, paying in leniency the price for the plea.[1]

Plea bargaining is the predominant way of settling criminal cases in the nation's big cities where most serious crime takes place. It is a little less prevalent in smaller communities, in part because their courts are not as overcrowded as in big cities, and in part because local newspapers focus the bright light of publicity very closely on the activities of courts in small communities. Plea bargaining takes place most readily when it is hidden by "the shield of anonymity afforded by life in the big city," as a New York County district attorney put it.

That shield is so effective in New York City that, in 1974, of 101,748 felony cases, 81,351 were settled by pleas in the lower criminal courts. These lower courts are not empowered to judge felonies. Their jurisdiction extends only to misdemeanors that may be punished by a maximum sentence of up to a year in jail and a fine of $1,000. A defendant facing twenty or thirty years in prison on multiple charges of robbery and possession of a gun may plead guilty to petit larceny and may be sentenced to two months in jail.

It would be very misleading to suggest that the reduction of 80 percent of New York City's felony cases to misdemeanors in plea bargaining reflects excessive leniency in all those cases, or even in the majority of those cases. The awareness that the case will be settled by plea bargaining leads many prosecutors to lodge excessive charges against defendants. This increases the pressure on defendants to accept the bargains offered to them by the prosecutor. Once the principle of plea bargaining is accepted, it is hard to fault the hagglers for little tricks of this sort.

One prosecutorial trick for pressuring defendants to accept a plea is high bail. In using this device, prosecutors are generally abetted by judges who know that the defendant behind bars because of inability to afford bail is far readier to accept a plea than the person at liberty while awaiting disposition of his case. The plea offered a defendant often lets him out of jail with a sentence equivalent to the time already served. Insisting on his innocence and going to trial will only prolong the amount of time the defendant must spend in jail. Moreover, if he is in jail while awaiting trial, the person probably won't be able to defend himself very well at trial. If there are witnesses who could help clear him, the defendant must generally visit them himself to persuade them to come forward at trial. If the defendant must sit in jail waiting for trial, he is forced to rely on an overburdened public defender or legal aid lawyer to round up witnesses. And, more likely than not, the defense lawyer will be pressuring the client to accept the plea and spare everybody the trouble of trial and spare the defendant the possibility of a long prison sentence. Only the most foolhardy of criminal defendants would insist on an actual trial in such circumstances. Guilt or innocence becomes quite irrelevant.

Many defense lawyers are vigorous supporters of plea bargaining. They perceive it as a necessary way of modifying the harshness of the criminal law. New York State law, for example, provides a minimum sentence of between fifteen and twenty-five years for the crime of murder, which must be served in prison before a murderer becomes eligible for parole. The law's definition of murder may well fit the case of a woman with no previous criminal record who kills her husband for belittling her sexual adequacy and comparing it unfavorably with other women he has known. Prosecutor and defense attorney alike will agree that the charge should be reduced to manslaughter because they can see little rational purpose for a fifteen-year minimum term in such a case.

The Supreme Court of the United States has given its blessings to plea bargaining. As the Court sees it, everybody wins with plea bargaining.

For a defendant who sees slight possibility of acquittal [the Court said in the 1970 case of *Brady* v. *United States*], the advantages of pleading guilty and limiting the probable penalty are obvious—his exposure is reduced, the correctional processes can begin immediately, and the practical burdens of a trial are eliminated. For the State there are also advantages—the more promptly imposed punishment after an admission of guilt may more effectively attain the objective of punishment; and with the avoidance of trial, scarce judicial and prosecutorial resources are conserved for those cases in which there is a substantial issue of the defendant's guilt or in which there is substantial doubt that the State can sustain its burden of proof. It is this mutuality of advantage that perhaps explains the fact that at present well over three-fourths of the criminal convictions in this country rest on pleas of guilty.

While plea bargaining ordinarily hides from public view, one recent case thrust it into the public spotlight. It was the case of Spiro Agnew. His prosecutors secured the return of the Vice-Presidency of the United States in exchange for a plea of nolo contendere and a $10,000 fine.

The Agnew case demonstrates one of the evils of plea bargaining. It was undignified. It reduced the moral ceremony that ought to be the consequence of crime to a bit of bartering more appropriate to the thieves' market in Baghdad. A few months after the sordid Agnew business, the nation witnessed a spectacle of extraordinary dignity: the impeachment hearings against Richard Nixon by the House Judiciary Committee. That solemn and deliberate proceeding had a purgative effect on the whole nation.

A criminal trial should be a time of extraordinary significance to a defendant, to the victim of a crime, and to the community at large. Guilt or innocence are, or should be, matters of great consequence. If the verdict is guilty, the imposition of punishment should be a dignified moral ceremony. Anything else depreciates the victim, the defendant, and the interest of justice.

The judges, prosecutors, and defense attorneys who manage the plea-bargaining process would mostly agree that some other way is better. They feel trapped, however, by the volume of cases and the need to arrive at rational settlements that may be impossible if the criminal law is enforced as it is written.

My proposals for abolishing certain kinds of crime would halve the volume faced by the criminal courts. In the previous chapter I proposed what I regard as a rational sentencing structure. Its adoption, I believe, addresses the other principal reason for present-day reliance on plea bargaining. Bail reform—to prohibit its use for de facto preventive detention—would also mitigate plea bargaining by reducing the pressure on defendants to plead guilty to crimes they may not have committed in exchange for sentences of time already served.

Even if these reforms were adopted, many courts would still be swamped by the number of trials to be held. Under such circumstances I see no alternative to the construction of additional physical facilities for trials and the hiring of more judges, prosecutors, and defense attorneys. The cost would be offset by not holding people in jail in preventive detention before they are convicted or acquitted.

Elimination of court overcrowding would pay many dividends. A witness to a crime who sits around all day waiting for a case to be called may refuse to return to court on the next scheduled date for a trial. The great delay between arrest and trial increases the pressure for preventive detention because it is feared the defendant will commit new crimes while awaiting trial. And the plea bargaining that derives from overcrowding breeds a deep cynicism in almost all who participate in the process.

"Stuff and nonsense" was Alice in Wonderland's response to the idea that the sentence should come first and the verdict and trial later. Plea bargaining carries the logic of the Queen of Hearts one step farther. It is sentence first, and never mind about the trial and verdict. They are simply eliminated from the system.

13

Unexplained and Unfair Sentencing

In his *Genealogy of Morals*,[1] Friedrich Nietzsche compiled a list of the various justifications for punishment:

1. Punishment administered with the view of rendering the offender harmless and preventing his doing further damage.

2. Punishment consisting of the payment of damages to the injured fairly, including affect compensation.

3. Punishment as the isolation of a disequilibrating agent, in order to keep the disturbance from spreading further.

4. Punishment as a means of inspiring fear of those who determine and execute it.

5. Punishment as cancellation of the advantages the culprit has heretofore enjoyed (as when he is put to work in the mines).

6. Punishment as the elimination of a degenerate element (or, as in Chinese law, a whole stock; as a means of keeping the race pure, or of maintaining a social type).

7. Punishment as a "triumph," the violating and deriding of an enemy finally subdued.

8. Punishment as a means of creating memory, either for the one who suffers it—so-called "improvement"—or for the witnesses.

9. Punishment as the payment of a fee, exacted by the authority which protects the evildoer from the excesses of vengeance.

10. Punishment as a compromise with the tradition of

160

vendetta, to the extent that this is still maintained and invoked as a privilege by powerful clans.

11. Punishment as a declaration of war, a warlike measure, against an enemy of peace, order, and authority.

Each rationale for punishment on Nietzsche's list, comprising everything from rehabilitation (number 8) to the final solution (number 6), probably turns up sooner or later as the basis for a criminal sentence by an American judge. The "exquisite agony" of it all, in Judge Marvin Frankel's words, is that the prisoner almost never knows the judge's reasons for imposing a particular punishment.

As matters stand today, in most American jurisdictions, defendants do not even see reports about them compiled by probation departments for submission to a judge before sentencing. These reports are often crowded with error and bias. If the defendant stoutly maintains his innocence despite his conviction, it may be held against him. The punishment he receives may be for not showing remorse (like Meursault in Camus's *The Stranger*), even though he did nothing that should make him feel remorse. Yet such pre-sentence reports, free of the questioning and testing that go on in a trial, may make the difference between a suspended sentence and five years in prison.

The United States Supreme Court considered the problem of pre-sentence reports in a 1949 case, *Williams* v. *New York*. Williams was sentenced to death, even though the jury that found him guilty of murder recommended life imprisonment. At sentencing, the judge said he rejected the jury's recommendation because the pre-sentence investigation revealed things about Williams that were important to the question of punishment but that the jury should not consider in its assessment of guilt. The pre-sentence report told the judge that Williams had committed some thirty burglaries "in and about the vicinity" where the murder was committed (Williams had not been convicted of any of those burglaries). The judge also concluded, on the basis of the pre-sentence report, that Williams was guilty of "a morbid sexuality."

In a decision written by the late Justice Hugo Black, the

Supreme Court affirmed the death penalty for Williams. "We cannot say that the due process clause renders a sentence void merely because a judge gets additional out-of-court information to assist him in the exercise of this awesome power of imposing the death penalty." The Justice made it clear that the Supreme Court's attitude toward pre-sentence reports was rooted in its view of their benevolent purpose.

Reformation and rehabilitation of offenders have become important goals of criminal jurisprudence. Modern changes in the treatment of offenders make it more necessary now than a century ago for observance of the distinction in the evidential procedure in the trial and sentencing processes [Black wrote]. Probation workers making reports of their investigation have not been trained to prosecute but to aid offenders. . . . To deprive sentencing judges of this kind of information would undermine modern penological procedural policies . . . most of the information now relied upon by judges to guide them in the intelligent imposition of sentences.

And so, in the interests of "reformation and rehabilitation," Williams was executed without ever getting an opportunity to challenge the information that meant the difference between life and death for him.

The principal argument for not allowing defendants to see pre-sentence reports is that informants will not speak honestly about a defendant if what they say will be told to him. But this fear seems no greater justification for denying a defendant the right to see a pre-sentence report than for denying a defendant the right to hear what a witness against him says in court. The pre-sentence report may have the more serious consequences.

Perhaps the most important way to relieve the "exquisite agony" of not knowing the reason for a particular sentence would be to require judges to write opinions explaining their sentences. The circumstances of crime vary enough so it isn't possible to spell out in legislation the exact punishment for each crime. Some discretion must be left with judges, though it need not be as much as they have today. But discretion need not be lawless. The exercise of discretion should be explained.

The need for explanations is of greatest significance when a defendant is convicted of what I call a public crime of violence and a judge metes out a sentence of 10, 12, or 15 years in prison. The defendant should have the opportunity to challenge the judge's interpretation of the circumstances of the crime just as he has an opportunity to defend himself against the charge that he committed the crime. In the absence of a statement of the reasons for a sentence, this is impossible.

Psychiatrist Willard Gaylin has explored the disparities in sentencing practices between judges of different temperament, philosophy, and geography.[2] Gaylin notes that in Oregon, 18 of 33 Selective Service violators were put on probation, and none got a prison term of longer than 3 years. By contrast, in southern Texas, 16 of 16 Selective Service violators got prison terms, 15 of them for over 3 years, and 14 of them for the full 5 years allowable under the law. Texas ideas of justice are further illustrated by a story Gaylin attributes to Judge Edward Lumbard. "A visitor to a Texas court," Lumbard told a conference of judges, "was amazed to hear the judge impose a suspended sentence where a man had pleaded guilty to manslaughter. A few minutes later, the same judge sentenced a man who pleaded guilty to stealing a horse, and gave him life imprisonment. When the judge was asked by the visitor about the disparity between the two sentences, he replied, 'Well, down here there is some men that need killin', but there ain't no horses that need stealin'."

Drawing on his experience as director of the Federal Bureau of Prisons for twenty-seven years, James V. Bennett gathered many examples of gross inequities in sentences.[3] Bennett describes a case of a thirty-two-year-old unemployed man whose wife had just suffered a miscarriage. They needed money for food and rent. Although the man had no previous criminal record, a Federal judge sentenced him to 15 years in prison for forging a government check. "This court," Bennett quotes the judge as saying, "intends to stop the stealing and forging of government checks."

In the same year, another Federal judge in the same circuit imposed a sentence of 30 days in jail for a similar crime. Bennett adds stories about a judge who hated tax offenders and was able to aggregate sentences for violations of the tax laws to add up to 177 months in prison, and of a mail robber sentenced to 15 years on a first offense and another to 5 years because he shouted at the judge. Bennett contrasts the extended prison sentences for possession of marijuana with 6-month suspended sentences for three pharmaceutical company scientists who held back and falsified test data on a drug that hurt hundreds of people.

In an effort to rationalize sentencing, Bennett proposed "sentencing institutes." The idea was to bring together the judges in an area to discuss their sentencing theories and practices with each other. The first such institute was held in 1959. "Sentencing councils" are another relatively recent innovation. The councils bring together probation officers and judges in an area to review recommendations for sentences by trial judges before the sentences are imposed. While the trial judge can reject the views of his colleagues, the discussions tend to circumscribe extreme disparities in sentencing. Although they are now fairly popular in the Federal courts, neither sentencing institutes nor sentencing councils are in use in most state court systems where the great majority of criminals are sentenced.

If judicial discretion were fettered by the need to explain punishments, regular appellate review of sentences would follow. Variations resulting from geography, tastes, and personalities would be greatly diminished if all sentences could be appealed and if higher courts reviewed the explanations offered by lower courts.

These days, appellate review of sentences is rare. When it happens, it is generally because judges have gratuitously offered their reasons for particular sentences and included impermissible considerations, as when a New Jersey judge cited an antiwhite poem by LeRoi Jones (Imamu Baraka) as the reason for giving him an extended prison term.

One such case in 1960 produced a trial judge's vigorous

denunciation of appellate review of sentencing. A court of appeals reversed the three-year prison term imposed on a defendant named Wiley. He had been convicted along with four other men of transporting stolen goods across state lines. "In view of the fact that the trial was expedited by waiving a jury and by stipulation of the various items that expedited the proof," Chief Judge William Campbell of the Federal District Court in Chicago said at sentencing, "I make the sentence less than I otherwise would. . . . Had there been a plea of guilty in this case, probably probation might have been considered under certain terms, but you are all aware of the standing policy here that once a defendant stands trial that element of grace is removed from the consideration of the Court in the imposition of sentence."

Campbell's naked confession that the price of a reduced sentence was giving up the right to trial by jury didn't figure in the court of appeals reversal of the sentence. The reversal was based on Campbell's effort to coerce guilty pleas by denying probation to Wiley or any other defendant who exercised the right to stand trial. The court of appeals sent the case back to Campbell for resentencing, pointing out that although Wiley was a minor participant in the crime and the only one of the five defendants without a record of prior convictions, he had received a longer sentence than any of the other defendants. Campbell took the occasion of resentencing to denounce appellate review.

As Campbell saw it, the whole procedure was "a waste of valuable time, effort and money." Then there was the problem of "the information contained in the reports of government investigators, which is not in the record." It "is highly confidential," Campbell said, "since otherwise it would be impossible for government investigators to continue certain investigations or gain confidential information about a defendant. If the trial judge is in part motivated by the reports of the government investigators in denying probation in a given case, he cannot in good conscience divulge this information . . . there is likewise the danger that the secrecy of the presentence investigation will also yield to the pressure of appellate review."

Campbell explained how the pre-sentence reports influenced his original sentencing of Wiley. "There is ample evidence in the reports of the government investigators, which are not a part of this record, but which I thoroughly considered before the imposition of sentence, that Wiley was involved in a similar offense, the burglary of the Chicago Terminal of Super Service Motor Freight Company . . . I think it is clear from the reports of the government investigators that Wiley perjured himself when he testified that he had never helped to dispose of any other stolen merchandise."

Campbell repeated his view that the denial of probation to Wiley was "rightfully motivated in part by the fact that he stood trial." Explaining his views further, Campbell said that "In sentencing Wiley, I seriously considered his prospects for rehabilitation. When he originally changed his plea from guilty to not guilty, there was no remorse in this man. McGhee, Kelley, Jackson and Helen [the other defendants] pled guilty and did stand conscience-stricken in repentance before the Court." The whole business of appellate review was a "dangerous precedent" to Campbell. "In good conscience and with due regard to my oath of office I cannot conclude that any sentence less than three years is either just or proper in the case of Wiley now before me. Accordingly, I hereby now again impose my original sentence of three years. However, out of my deep respect for the Court of Appeals, and in obedience to its mandate, I also hereby suspend the execution of the said sentence. The defendant Wiley may go hence without delay."

It is hard to think of a stronger argument for appellate review of sentencing than this denunciation of it by Chief Judge Campbell. He refused to consider probation because Wiley pled innocent and stood trial. This also proved to Campbell that Wiley had no remorse, though remorse should hardly be expected of a defendant who says he is innocent. The sentence was largely based on a crime other than the one for which Wiley was convicted, a burglary he had never been charged with committing. Wiley never had a chance to defend himself against the charge that determined the prison term, much less was it proved. If the defendant subsequent to Wiley had the cheek to exercise his right to trial by jury, he could expect even harsher treatment from Campbell.

More of the nation's judges resemble Campbell than Marvin Frankel. But the defendants they sentence are entitled to know why one convict gets off with a suspended sentence or probation and another goes behind bars for long years. In the nightmare world of Franz Kafka's story "In the Penal Colony," a prisoner is never informed of his sentence. There is only a brief moment of awareness for the prisoner just before death on the "Harrow," a diabolical machine that slowly tattoos the sentence on a prisoner's back with vibrating needles that cut ever deeper into the flesh. "How quiet he grows at just about the sixth hour!" a prison officer explains to a visitor to the penal colony. "Enlightenment comes to the most dull-witted. It begins around the eyes. From there it radiates. A moment that might tempt one to get under the Harrow oneself. Nothing more happens than that the man begins to understand the inscription, he purses his mouth as if he were listening. You have seen how difficult it is to decipher the script with one's eyes; but our man deciphers it with his wounds."

Not knowing the reasons for a sentence is not quite so Kafkaesque as not knowing the sentence itself, but it is the next thing to it. Eventually, prisoners may decipher the reasons through their wounds. But must enlightenment be left to that?

Articulation of the reasons for sentencing would permit systematic appellate review and thereby eliminate some of the most bizarre disparities in punishment. By removing the shroud of secrecy from sentencing, it would allow the development of agreed-upon criteria for punishment. Those criteria might serve the ends of public safety and fairness better than the crazy quilt of punishment theories prevalent today. We could hardly do much worse.

14
Prison and Alternatives

John Ehrlichman's lawyer, Ira Lowe, stood before Judge John Sirica and asked that his client be permitted to work in a public-service job as an alternative to imprisonment. Ehrlichman wanted to serve as a lawyer for the Pueblo Indian Council in New Mexico, a task he was especially suited for because of his knowledge of land-use law. The publicity led the Pueblo Indian Council to disclaim any interest in Ehrlichman. But in raising the question, John Ehrlichman performed a very useful role.

It was said that Ehrlichman's sudden interest in putting his talents to use on behalf of the Pueblo Indians was self-serving. Perhaps so. It does not diminish the value of drawing national attention to the issue of alternatives to prison.

Lowe described to Judge Sirica the case of a doctor convicted of illegally dispensing narcotics. His sentence was to serve as the only doctor for four thousand nonpaying residents of Tombstone, Arizona. He is "not costing the taxpayers a peso," Lowe told Sirica, "he is not rehabilitating himself by staring at the walls or writing letters to his lawyer trying to get out, and his family is not adrift to suffer."

Alternatives to prison present many very difficult problems. While it was probably good to make the doctor serve the residents of Tombstone, and it would have been equally good for John

168

Ehrlichman to serve his sentence as a lawyer for the Pueblo Indians, it is difficult to distribute such punishments equitably. Ehrlichman and the doctor in Tombstone might derive great satisfaction from performing such work. Criminals without the benefit of training as lawyers or doctors might be able to perform only less satisfying, menial tasks. Is the answer that Ehrlichman and the doctor should also perform menial jobs if they are to be allowed alternate service? Should they have to serve, say, as orderlies in a mental hospital? Presumably, any such service should be unpleasant if it is to deter people from crime. Perhaps alternate-service jobs should be similar even though the skills of criminals are not similar.

There are other problems. John Ehrlichman would not be likely to walk away from the Pueblo Indian Council and simply disappear. He is too recognizable to get very far unless he wants to live a life as furtive as Patricia Hearst, and even she couldn't do it forever. Nor is it likely the doctor would run away from Tombstone. He has family ties and a professional career to resume. But what about the nineteen-year-old convicted of burglary who would just as soon get away from his parents and has established no family of his own? Wouldn't he simply abscond if assigned unpleasant public-service work instead of prison? Again, it would be grossly inequitable to deny that young man alternate service while permitting a John Ehrlichman to enjoy something resembling a *Festungshaft*, the relatively pleasant detention imposed on Hitler and other Nazis convicted of crimes in the Weimar period. The problem of equity is not insuperable, but it will have to be reckoned with if we are to make extensive use of public-service work as an alternative to prison. Public service seems eminently sensible as a punishment for property crime, or for the kind of crime committed by John Ehrlichman. Since I believe the state should compensate victims of property crime, it seems only fair that the criminal compensate the state.[1] As for Ehrlichman, his crime was against the whole public. In fairness, he should perform services for the whole public.

A variation on the idea of public service is restitution to the victim. The Federal Law Enforcement Assistance Administration is now funding restitution programs in Georgia, Iowa, and Minnesota.

While restitution is an ancient concept, in our time it was reintroduced largely through the efforts of David Fogel, the commissioner of corrections for Minnesota from 1971 to 1973. Here is how the Minnesota Restitution Center works. Men and women convicted of property crimes, chosen at random, sign contracts. The contracts require them to live at the Restitution Center for a period of up to a year, get a job, and use part of what they earn to repay the victims of their crimes. For male criminals, living quarters are on one floor of the Minneapolis YMCA building. For women enrolled in the program, living quarters are a cottage on the prison grounds. From there, they travel to work every day.

Before signing restitution contracts, criminals are required to meet their victims face-to-face. For some of the criminals, this is said to be a very moving experience. (Perhaps it also is for the victims.) Some advocates of restitution programs are particularly enthusiastic about these meetings. By making criminals confront their victims as individual human beings, they hope to diminish recidivism.

Restitution programs are too new and too few to evaluate whether they reduce recidivism. Even if they do not have that impact, they seem a very good idea. Victims are compensated, and people who commit property crimes are treated less harshly than if they were confined full-time in prisons. Then, too, it costs the state a lot less to provide dormitory space in a YMCA building than to confine the same people in heavily guarded, fortress-like prisons. A few criminals (remember, they are picked at random) have absconded from the restitution programs, but not so many as to cancel out the other advantages.

A system substantially relying on fines instead of prison is hopelessly inequitable. A fine of $1,000 is enormous to some, minuscule to others. It is like allowing the rich and the poor the equal right to sleep under the bridges of Paris. Nor would a fine based on net worth solve the problem. Some people, probably the very rich and the very poor, would find it relatively painless to part with 10 percent or 50 percent of their net worth. It would not change their life-styles. By contrast, many people in the middle class would find a fine of a large proportion of their net worth very painful.

Fines do serve a valuable purpose in curbing traffic violations. It is not the amount of money involved, however, that deters violators. Most people who own automobiles can readily afford the relatively small amounts of money they are required to pay for traffic tickets. The deterrent effect derives more from the nuisance of arranging to pay the fine, the possibility that an accumulation of moving offenses will cost the driver a license, and the baleful stare of the policeman who writes the ticket.

While fines have some attraction as a method of enforcing laws against very low level crimes, it is worth noting the objection raised by Herbert Packer. "The more indiscriminate we are in treating conduct as criminal," Packer observed, "the less stigma resides in the mere fact that a man has been convicted of something called a crime." Rather than dilute the force of the criminal sanction, he argued, we should "forego primary reliance on such devices as monetary fines. If the most that we are prepared to exact in the great majority of occurrences of a particular form of reprehended conduct is the payment of money into the public treasury, we should not impose on ourselves the manifold burdens of invoking the criminal sanction." [2]

There is also a constitutional problem. The United States Supreme Court recently put an end to the ancient and unfair practice of holding in prison people who could not pay their fines. The absurdity of putting such people behind bars was noted in Justice William Brennan's opinion for the Court. "Imprisonment in such a case," he wrote, "is not imposed to further any penal objective of the State. It is imposed to augment the State's revenues but obviously does not serve that purpose; the defendant cannot pay because he is indigent and his imprisonment, rather than aiding collection of the revenue, saddles the state with the cost of feeding and housing him for the period of imprisonment."

The principal contemporary alternative to prison is probation. It had its origins in the mid-nineteenth century when wealthy Boston businessman John Augustus was in court one day and took an interest in a defendant charged as a "common drunkard." Augustus persuaded the judge to release the man on probation in his custody, took the man home, gave him fresh clothes, fed him, and got him a job. Several weeks later, Augustus brought the man back to court completely changed in appearance and manner. The judge was so impressed he let the sometime drunkard off with a fine of one cent.

Over the next eighteen years, until his death in 1859, John Augustus obtained custody of nearly two thousand persons. At the start, all were drunks but, as time went on, increasing numbers were those who had committed more serious crimes. Even so, Augustus apparently achieved great success, much more than is claimed for any subsequent probation program. Few of Augustus's charges committed new crimes, and only a handful are reported to have run away.

Today, probation has been adopted by all fifty states. There are many more people on probation than behind bars. They have been sentenced to continue living in the community, but subject to supervision. Sometimes the conditions of probation are onerous, sometimes not. Some probation officers have light case loads and spend a lot of time with the convicts assigned to them. More commonly, probation officers are responsible for a hundred or more cases at a time. They see their charges on brief, periodic visits and keep tabs on whether they change addresses or lose jobs. Occasionally, they investigate probationers to discover whether they have violated such conditions of probation as prohibitions on driving a car, drinking, extramarital sex, traveling beyond fixed boundaries, late hours, or keeping bad company. Sometimes probationers are required to go to church, continue living with their wives, or keep up child-support payments. Any connection between these things and the particular crime the person committed is often remote if it exists at all. The conditions of probation may reflect the tastes and prejudices of a judge more than anything else.

In its *Guides for Sentencing,* the National Probation and Parole Association states a rationale for probation. "Far more effective than deterrence as an objective of sentencing," the association claims, "is rehabilitation, the satisfactory adjustment of the offender to law-abiding society. Whether it takes the form of probation—proved to be the most practical approach where circumstances warrant its use—or of commitment and ultimately parole, it is based on the principle that the best way to protect society is to change convicted offenders into law-abiding citizens."

In practice, the rehabilitation purpose claimed by the National Probation and Parole Association is not the only rationale employed by judges in determining whether to employ probation. The motives for probation are often as obscure and as intermingled as for a prison sentence. Probation is used as a way of rewarding a police informant, as a method of permitting a convicted person to work and make restitution, or as a way to allow a criminal to support his family. It may be used as a method of encouraging guilty pleas (apparently its purpose in the sentencing of Spiro Agnew). Sometimes it is used because there isn't enough room to house any more people in the jails, and probation may also be employed as a relatively mild punishment for first offenders or for people who have committed relatively minor crimes.

As far as its avowed purpose of rehabilitation is concerned, I think probation may be effective only in the sense that it keeps out of prison some people whose lives should not be so badly disrupted. There is no evidence that probation rehabilitates people any more than if people were simply left alone. Probation is punitive, however, and its principal use should be as an alternative to prison for people who have committed minor crimes and who deserve some punishment.

I part company with those who would like to spend a great

deal more money on probation. Their hope is that better probation officers with smaller case loads will spend more time counseling and guiding their charges. If that means getting them jobs, or getting them into schools or training programs, fine (though the money could probably be better spent creating more jobs for probationers instead of jobs for probation officers). If it means more counseling without getting them more jobs, as is likely, it is probably wasteful. Quite enough money is presently spent on probation for it to serve well as a low-level punishment. That, I suggest, is what probation is and the way it should be perceived.

Corporal punishment is another possible alternative to prison. While contemporary prisons were devised as less cruel alternatives to the stocks, branding, or flogging, are prisons really less cruel? It seems to me a very difficult question.

For myself, I have no doubt I would prefer the stocks for a week, or forty lashes, than prison for six months or a year. Yet the prospect of the stocks or a whipping is sufficiently frightening and humiliating to be a considerable deterrent. If corporal punishment seems preferable to prison and is still a deterrent, why not opt for it? At any rate, why not allow a prisoner a choice?

Before answering the question, let me present it in more extreme form. I have advocated lengthy prison sentences as punishment for some kinds of violent crime. The purpose is to prevent the criminal from committing additional crimes of violence during the years in prison. Suppose the criminal opted for the alternative of being blinded, or having his hands chopped off, or (in the case of a rapist) being castrated? Maiming would incapacitate the criminal quite as effectively as a long prison sentence. Since incapacitation is the purpose of such long sentences, if the prisoner prefers it, why isn't maiming a permissible alternative?

My objection to corporal punishment is, in Beccaria's words, "the example of barbarity it presents." To the victim of corporal punishment, it may be less barbarous than ten years, a year, or even a month behind bars. But an overriding purpose of the criminal law should be to prevent citizens from committing physical violence against each other. It cannot be useful to that end for the state to set an example of violence against its own citizens. If prison is more barbarous to the victim, at least citizens cannot readily mimic the state by holding other citizens behind bars.

Even suggesting corporal punishment or maiming as alternatives to prison may seem bizarre. Yet the question arose in California in 1975. Two convicted child molesters, Joseph Kenner and Paul de la Haye, asked that they be castrated as an alternative to the probability of life in prison. They obtained the consent of their sentencing judge, Douglas P. Woodworth. The operations were blocked when the urologist who had planned to perform them was told by colleagues at University Hospital in San Diego that he opened himself to a lawsuit for assault and battery and he might not be covered for it by standard malpractice insurance. The same advice was given the doctor at a general meeting of the San Diego County Urological Society.

Castration is no longer prevalent. The last reported case of its use as an alternative to long-term confinement in prison was in Colorado in 1972. I do not know how often it was used in the past. Statistics don't seem to be available. But there were several hundred cases in California in this century, and it was used with some frequency in several of the states. The same results are now sought through more up-to-date methods, perhaps more humane, perhaps not. Some of these shiny new methods were a major topic of discussion at a March 1975 meeting of the American Psychopathological Association.

Dr. John Money of Johns Hopkins Medical Center presented a paper at the psychopathologists' meeting describing the treatment of sex offenders with injections of a drug known as Depo-Provera. The drug apparently diminishes a man's ability to have erections, ejaculations, and erotic fantasies. According to Money, although the Johns Hopkins Ethics Committee forbade the use of Depo-Provera on prisoners, he had received letters from sex-offending inmates "virtually begging" to be treated with the drug. Denying these prisoners Depo-Provera while in prison, said Money, condemns them to "the vindictive treatment of serving [a] jail sentence" and makes impossible "compassionate treatment."

Other scientists have proposed such forms of "compassionate treatment" as behavior modification, psychosurgery, electroconvulsive therapy (ECT), and electronic stimulation of the brain (EST). These "treatments" should not require extensive consideration when they produce physical pain and are avowedly compulsory. Such was the case with the START (Special Training and Rehabilitation Treatment) program for Federal prisoners at the United States Medical Center in Springfield, Missouri. An ACLU attorney, Arpiar Saunders, who visited the program, subsequently wrote to the director of the center, Dr. Pasquale J. Ciccone, describing how it modified the behavior of Gerard Wilson and Alvin Gagne. They

were shackled by their arms and legs by means of leather and metal straps and chains to their steel beds ... on several occasions in the five days they had been shackled, they had been forced to eat with both hands still shackled to the bed and had experienced great difficulty in receiving staff assistance in removing the chains in order to perform necessary bodily functions.... [N]either individual [Saunders continued] was ever charged with or made an appearance before a disciplinary committee for violation of a rule or regulation.

The START program, discontinued in the face of litigation brought by Saunders and his colleagues in the National Prison Project, was out-and-out cruelty. Many state laws already prohibit psychosurgery and ECT in the absence of consent. It seems likely that compulsory programs like START, involving severe aversive conditioning, will also be outlawed by statute or court decision. The courts can probably also be counted upon, ultimately, to do away with such institutions as Patuxent.

For the past twenty years, Maryland has imprisoned people it regards as defective delinquents at the Patuxent Institution. It is headed by a psychiatrist and has a large staff of psychiatrists, psychologists, and social workers. The institution is a "great idea" to Dr. Karl Menninger, who expressed envy that there is not a similar institution in Kansas.

Almost any crime punishable by imprisonment qualifies a person for commitment to Patuxent. Once there, the prisoner is supposed to stay until a review committee, comprising psychiatrists, psychologists, and sociologists, decides he is cured. If that means spending a lifetime at Patuxent, so be it.

Until recent changes were made, a prisoner at Patuxent started out in solitary confinement in filthy conditions. Gradually, he would be promoted to more attractive quarters. If he did well, in the eyes of the institution's staff, he achieved very comfortable surroundings. If he did poorly, he was demoted, perhaps all the way back to solitary confinement. Doing well at Patuxent meant progressing through the institution's psychotherapeutic program.

Edward McNeil did very badly at Patuxent. He refused to talk to the psychiatrists. As a result, McNeil, who was convicted at the age of nineteen and sentenced to no more than five years in prison (which would have made him eligible for parole after serving a quarter of his sentence), spent six years in solitary confinement at Patuxent. His release was finally ordered by the United States Supreme Court because, as Justice Thurgood Marshall wrote, McNeil "is presently confined in Patuxent without any lawful authority to support that confinement. His sentence having expired, he is no longer within the class of persons eligible for commitment to the Institution as a defective delinquent." Prior to the *McNeil* decision in 1972, almost half the people committed to Patuxent stayed there longer than the maximum sentences they had received.

More difficult questions arise when intrusive therapeutic techniques are "voluntary." This problem was confronted in a 1973 court case in Detroit, *Kaimowitz and Doe* v. *Department of Mental Health for the State of Michigan.*

"John Doe," a man who had spent seventeen years in Ionia State Hospital as a criminally convicted "sexual psychopath," applied to be a subject of an experimental psychosurgery program. He signed an "informal consent" form, and his participation in the experiment was approved by both a scientific review committee and a human rights review committee. A legal services lawyer, Gabriel Kaimowitz, stepped in on his own and filed a taxpayer suit to stop the psychosurgery as against public policy and a violation of constitutional rights. The Michigan court agreed with Kaimowitz, stating that "incarceration diminishes the capacity to consent . . . [the inmate] is particularly vulnerable as a result of his mental condition, the deprivation stemming from involuntary confinement, and the effects of the phenomena of institutionalization." As the court saw it, "Institutionalization tends to strip the individual of the support which permits him to maintain his sense of self worth and the value of his mental integrity."

"John Doe" is now a free man, without psychosurgery. While the *Kaimowitz* case was in court, the "sexual psychopath" law was declared unconstitutional and "John Doe" was released.

An ACLU challenge to the behavior-modification program for convicted child molesters in Connecticut is still awaiting decision by a Federal court. It is a small program in use at the maximum-security prison at Somers, Connecticut. About a dozen "volunteers" at a time participate.

The Somers program is run by a young psychiatrist, Roger Wolfe. An American Bar Association–sponsored journal reports,

In the electric shock component of the program, the inmate lies on a couch facing a picture screen, his trousers and undershorts pulled down to his knees. A disc attached to a battery-powered device that produces shocks is strapped around his thigh, as close as possible to the genitals. A trained programmer shows slides of young boys or girls and adult men or women (depending on the inmate's sexual preferences) in provocative poses. When a picture of a child appears, the programmer gives the inmate a harmless but painful electric shock. No shock is administered when pictures of adults are flashed on the screen.[3]

Hypnosis is also used at Somers. "I ask the inmate to imagine walking down the street and seeing a little girl, nine years old, blonde hair," Wolfe told the ABA interviewer. The inmate, under hypnosis, is told to imagine fondling the girl and becoming sexually aroused. The child molester is then told "he is getting very nauseous . . . a huge horde of rats" is gnawing at him. "For some it's rats," said Wolfe, "and for others it might be castration with a branding iron." [4]

The ACLU lawsuit challenging the program at Somers was brought on behalf of a convicted child molester who did not volunteer to submit to Roger Wolfe's ministrations. This, the prisoner says, cost him the chance for parole. Officials of the Connecticut Parole Board admit that a participant in the behavior-modification program stands a better chance to be released from prison early. The other side of this coin is that an inmate who refuses to volunteer, like the ACLU's plaintiff, is held in prison longer for refusing to "volunteer."

Jessica Mitford has described an analogous problem: the widespread use of prisoners as experimental subjects by drug companies.[5] She found that despite the great harm they suffer, a third to a half of the inmates in many prisons have volunteered to be guinea pigs in these experiments. They volunteer, and waive any rights to collect damages if they suffer injuries, in the hope they will be let out of prison sooner and because they are paid one or two dollars a day as volunteers in these experiments. Tiny amounts of money loom very large to prisoners who earn a few cents an hour in prison jobs and are desperate for money to spend in the prison commissary. Then, there is the sheer boredom of prison life. It plays a part in persuading prisoners to volunteer for dangerous medical experiments.

Ms. Mitford advocates the standard of the Nuremberg War Crimes Tribunal to cover medical experiments. The court at Nuremberg ruled that "the person involved should have legal capacity to give consent; should be so situated as to be able to exercise free power of choice . . . and should have sufficient knowledge and comprehension of the elements of the subject matter involved as to enable him to make an understanding, enlightened decision." Even if the other criteria are met, it is plain prisoners are not "so situated as to be able to exercise free power of choice." That is true for drug experiments and it is equally true for psychosurgery and other methods of behavior modification.

Behavior-modification programs in prisons pose additional problems. Are they merely disguised punishments? Will they make prisoners more tractable to suit the needs of their guards, or will they make prisoners better able to function outside the prison? Whatever difficulties any other person might face in learning all the consequences of an operation, or drugs, or electric shocks, aren't the difficulties much greater in prison? What procedures could ensure the voluntariness of a prisoner's participation in a behavior-modification program?

Psychologist David Wexler has proposed that therapeutic techniques be ranked according to their intrusiveness. His ranking, from the least to the most intrusive, is "milieu therapy, psychotherapy, drug therapy, behavior modification, aversion therapy, electroconvulsive therapy, electronic stimulation of the brain, lobotomy, and stereotactic psychosurgery." [6] In this ranking, Wexler has considered the primary and side effects of the technique, the extent that an unwilling person can avoid the effects of the technique, and the extent of physical intrusion. Employing Wexler's continuum, I would argue that even when voluntary, everything more intrusive than psychotherapy should be excluded from prisons. Perhaps the therapeutic arts will advance to the point where they do not create zombies and are not painful, and the consequences are fully known and proved effective. Perhaps the availability of these therapies in prison can be divorced from decisions about release. Then it will be time to reconsider. For now, the more intrusive therapies cannot be considered reasonable alternatives to prison. They only add to the punishment of prison itself.

If most alternatives—at least for major crimes—seem worse than prison, can prisons be made better? Certainly. Loss of liberty is punishment enough to deter people from committing crime. And for the people I would put in prison for long periods, confinement is enough to prevent them from committing more crimes.

The basic characteristic of prisons will remain. In Erving Goffman's words, prisons are "total institutions." [7] Inmates are systematically stripped of their own sense of identity, regimented, mortified, and degraded.

Personal identity equipment is removed [Goffman points out], as well as other possessions with which the inmate may have identified himself. . . . As a substitute for what has been taken away, institutional issue is provided, but this will be the same for large categories of inmates and will be regularly repossessed by the institution. In brief, standardized defacement will occur. In addition, ego-invested separateness from fellow inmates is significantly diminished in many areas of activity, and tasks are prescribed that are *infra dignitatem.* Family, occupational, and educational career lives are chopped off, and a stigmatized status is substituted. Sources of fantasy materials which had meant momentary release from stress in the home world are denied. Areas of autonomous decision are eliminated through the process of collective scheduling of daily activity. Many channels of communication with the outside are restricted or closed off completely. Verbal discreditings occur in many forms as a matter of course. Expressive signs of respect for the staff are coercively and continuously demanded. And the effect of each of these conditions is multiplied by having to witness the mortification of one's fellow inmates.[8]

The best of prisons will retain these characteristics. But prisoners need not suffer the gratuitous cruelty of the prison system as we know it.

Prisoners should be able to make and receive telephone calls, correspond with outsiders as they see fit, obtain and read whatever literature they choose, and receive as many and as varied visitors as hospital patients. The restrictions on these things are legacies of the belief in prisons as places that rehabilitate their inmates by breaking their ties to a corrupt environment. Since that view of prisons should be discarded, the restrictions flowing from it should also be discarded.

I also advocate conjugal visits for prisoners. (I use the term to include all visits for purposes of sexual relations, whether or not these relations have been previously licensed by marriage.) Among American prisons, only the Mississippi State Penitentiary at Parchman permits conjugal visits for large numbers of prisoners. It has been going on there at least since 1918, and possibly as far back as when the prison opened in 1900. Apparently it began as an accommodation for black prisoners, who were thought to be little better than animals, with animal needs. White prisoners, segregated from blacks for most of Parchman's history, demanded equal rights, and the practice of conjugal visits was extended to them.

There is not a great deal of evidence whether the conjugal visit system at Parchman increases family stability or diminishes homosexual rape. Perhaps it does. Perhaps those claims for it are too great. But it must relieve some of the frustrations of prison life. That is reason enough to endorse it. While conjugal visits are common features of prison systems in other countries, as yet there has been only very limited experimental imitation of the Mississippi system elsewhere in the United States.

Prisoners should be paid the minimum wage for their labor in prison. This proposal will shock many people. Or it will produce the response it often elicits from prison officials: "Yes, and we'll deduct the cost of room and board." Since it costs $10,000 to $15,000 a year to keep a man in prison, deducting the cost of room and board would leave nothing.

I don't propose to deduct the cost of a prisoner's room. Prisoners are not in prison by choice. If the state deprives them of liberty, the state should bear the cost of housing them. The cost of board, or at least food, is something else. Outside or inside, prisoners have to eat. Right now, the food in prisons is terrible. It costs very little of the prison budget to feed prisoners—perhaps $1 a day. (Most of the cost of keeping people in prison is for the salaries of guards and administrative staff. One guard for every two prisoners is a common ratio.) Prisoners could be served and charged for their food cafeteria-style. If they chose to eat well, it would cost them. Of course, the prices would have to be monitored to ensure they were fair and not simply a device for recapturing all the pay prisoners would receive for their work.

Inmates of Tillberge Prison in Sweden, an institution not far from Stockholm, earn about 10 Swedish kroner (about $2.20) an hour for their work in a prison factory building prefabricated homes. Out of this, they must pay for their own food. Some of the remaining money is given to them to spend in prison, while most of it is held to be given to them on release. Swedish prison authorities are sufficiently pleased with the results of the Tillberge experiment to want to extend it to the country's other prisons.

At present, several American prison systems do rather nicely selling the products of prison labor. The Federal Prison Industries Corporation, established in 1935, has grossed more than $1 billion in its forty-year history. It has a profit picture that would be the envy of many private corporations. The state prison systems in California and Texas also make a lot of money. If it can be done in those systems, it can be done elsewhere. But instead of making money for state treasuries, the proceeds of prison industries should be used to pay convict labor. When the prisoner got out, he would probably have some savings and a lot better chance of setting himself up properly than if he left with the $40 or $50 customary today. The savings from labor in prison could hold him until he got a job, or even enable him to go into business. The $40 or $50 would enable him to do little more than purchase a gun.

Norval Morris has offered a number of sensible suggestions for the organization of a prison for repetitively violent criminals.[9] Since such people ought to comprise the greatest part of the prison population (because most other people don't belong in prison), I borrow a few of Morris's proposals to cover all prisons.

Like Morris, I think about 200 inmates the right size for a prison. It would be big enough to offer varied work within the prison and allow proper recreational facilities. At the same time, a prison of 200 inmates would not be so big as to exacerbate the loss of a sense of identity that necessarily accompanies incarceration. Most of all, the number 200 sounds best for permitting outsiders to monitor what is going on inside. It is virtually impossible for legislators, the press, or voluntary organizations to keep a watchful eye on giant institutions or on great numbers of tiny institutions.

Morris also proposes "the injection of women into the prison at all levels, including that of front of the line guard." This he argues, and I concur, "will tend to reduce violence. . . . As a matter of observation, men behave better in the presence of women. The social skills of many male offenders in dealing with women are distorted and underdeveloped. Frequent and constructive association with women as staff members of the prison will have a positive impact upon the prisoners' social relationships." [10]

Ideally, women prisoners should be housed in the same institutions as men. The problem, as Morris points out, is that there are very few women prisoners. Many of the women who are behind bars are there for prostitution, a crime I would abolish. Unless equality for women produces a great upsurge in crimes committed by women—something beginning to take place—the number of women available to be confined with men would be so disproportionately small as to make it preferable to continue segregation of prisoners by sex.

The prison envisioned by Morris would have "maximum security at its perimeter but with a great deal of privacy and freedom of movement within." Again, I agree. I think prisoners should have their own rooms (not barred cells) and should be able to lock other people out. Unless a prisoner has engaged in violence within the prison, however, I see no justification for allowing the prison to lock an inmate in his room. The practice of locking prisoners in their own cells and thereby preventing them from communicating with each other seems a legacy of the nineteenth-century belief in the curative consequences of isolation. In some of the very earliest prisons this was carried to the extreme of not allowing prisoners to talk to each other—even when they went into the same dining room for meals. Just as prisoners were to be rehabilitated by removal from the corrupting environment outside, they were to be isolated from each other so as not to corrupt each other. For the most part, contemporary prisons have given up on the idea that they can isolate prisoners from each other. Locking prisoners in their cells seems merely a thoughtless legacy from that earlier period.

By this time, the reader is familiar with my hostility to the idea that punishment and treatment can be combined. Nevertheless, I think there is a place for treatment in prisons. Inmates should be free to visit psychiatrists, psychotherapists, priests, or yoga instructors in prison. If the prisoners think these will do them good, fine. But the availability of treatment in the institution should play no part in sentencing or in any determination to release the prisoner.

In the next chapter, I advocate the abolition of parole. If that should happen, the problem of therapy coerced by the chance it will buy freedom would disappear. But in the more likely event parole is preserved, participation in a treatment program should have absolutely no weight in parole decisions. Unless this is done, treatment programs will become coercive and ineffective, though this is not my principal reason for opposing coerced treatment. I fear coerced treatment because it leads inevitably to imprisoning people for their own good, something I consider grossly unfair, as well as probably futile.

People should be put in prison, if at all, only for the good of others. Those who put them there have a responsibility to minimize the pain of prison. That is why I advocate sex, wages, privacy, and freedom of movement within prisons for prisoners. Some will object that the prisons I envision would be so comfortable that people would commit crimes to get in. That happens. Some people who have spent virtually all their lives in institutions don't know how to survive outside. They deliberately violate parole or commit robberies with toy guns and then wait for the police to catch them. Prisons—even prisons with tiny, barred cells, open toilets, and twenty-four-hour lights shining into cells—offer them more security than the unknown world outside.

A few wretches may prefer life in prison. But it is hardly

credible that people who would not otherwise commit crimes would do so because a few amenities have been added to prison existence. The prisons I propose resemble *sharaskas*, the elite prisons described in Alexander Solzhenitsyn's novel *The First Circle*. They are not in the very worst part of Hell, as Solzhenitsyn's title tells us. Nevertheless, they are in Hell. The highly speculative fear that prison would be so attractive that people would commit crimes to get in is no excuse for maintaining the barbarous conditions now prevalent.

Most of the reforms I propose are already in use in Sweden. Concededly, comparisons between Sweden and the United States are extremely difficult. Sweden's entire population is about equal to that of New York City. The country is racially homogeneous, has eliminated all extreme poverty, and by American standards has little serious crime. Most of the 4,000 or so inmates of its prisons—a declining number—were convicted of drunk driving or larceny. Only a small minority of Sweden's prisoners have committed violent crimes. These differences make changes of the sort I propose far simpler and far less risky in Sweden than they could possibly be in the United States. The Swedish example must be mentioned, however, because it is a working success. Its basic operating principle is opposite to the philosophy that has guided American prisons since their founding a century and a half ago. The Swedes are trying to disrupt as little as possible the prisoner's ties with the community he has left behind, and—by allowing inmates to maintain conjugal relationships and earn money—are trying to enable prisoners to reenter those communities as easily as possible after leaving prison.

With all its faults, prison still seems the best alternative for punishing serious crimes of violence. We should limit its use and employ public service, restitution, and probation to punish a great deal of property crime. When we must use prisons, we should minimize the pain they cause.

15

Eliminate Parole and God Playing

At the age of twenty, Charles R. went to prison. His crime: interstate transportation of a stolen vehicle. He had been drinking and, together with a friend, stole a car in an effort to leave home. Because of his age, Charles was sentenced under the Federal Youth Corrections Act to an indeterminate term of up to six years in prison.

In prison, Charles was attacked homosexually. Several times. He asked to be put in an isolation cell for his own protection. The request was granted, and he was locked up twenty-four hours a day.

Several months later, Charles R. got a chance to go before the parole board. The examiner for the board informed Charles his application for parole would not be considered unless he first returned to the general prison population. It seems the prison rules didn't allow a prisoner in isolation to participate in correctional programs.

The origins of parole are traced to the shipment of indentured felons from England and Ireland to the crown colonies. Starting in about the middle of the seventeenth century, felons

187

were granted pardons on the condition that they sail to America in the custody of shipmasters who sold them to the highest bidders to be servants for specified periods. The Revolutionary War ended the availability of the American Colonies, but newly discovered Australia was quickly substituted as a place to accommodate released convicts.

A governor of a penal colony off the coast of Australia in the 1840s, Alexander Maconochie, refined the concept of parole. He experimented with a system of marks or credits for good behavior and work in prison. The marks earned by a prisoner shortened his term of incarceration. And as the prisoner approached his release date, Maconochie gave him more and more freedom in order to prepare the convict for the outside world.

Parole first appeared in the United States at Elmira Reformatory in New York State in the 1870s. In a system that is the direct ancestor of the Federal Youth Corrections Act under which Charles R. was sentenced, youths were given sentences of up to six years. Elmira's Board of Managers was authorized to parole any such prisoner before completion of sentence. Once paroled, the convict was required to adhere to certain conditions and to submit to supervision. Failure to obey the rules meant return to the reformatory.

A few years later, the system was extended to adults. By the early part of the twentieth century, parole had been adopted in almost every American state. Of about 200,000 convicted adults in American prisons,[1] about 70 percent are eligible for parole in any year. About 50,000 persons a year are granted parole. Sixty percent of all prisoners are paroled before completing their sentences.

Quite obviously, a parole board's decisions are enormously important to prisoners. The decisions mean the difference between freedom (subject to the conditions of parole) and additional months or years behind bars. A parole board's decisions also mean the difference between letting loose among the rest of us some people who have committed heinous crimes, or keeping them locked up at enormous cost to them and us. These are decisions to be made according to well-thought-out criteria after thorough study and deliberation. Right?

Wrong—at least in practice.

"The eight members of the U.S. Board of Parole make 17,000 decisions each year," notes Alvin Bronstein, director of the ACLU's National Prison Project. "On the average, the board has to consider about 325 applications a week. When you take away time for administrative duties and for travel to the more than 40 federal prisons throughout the country, the members are left about three minutes for each of their expertly reasoned decisions." [2]

In November 1973, the United States Board of Parole published for the first time a series of guidelines to give prisoners information on their chances for being paroled. The issuance of the guidelines was prompted by a Federal court decision by Judge June L. Green, who ruled, in an ACLU National Prison Project case, that the United States Board of Parole is a rule-making agency and could be compelled to publish its decisions in the *Federal Register.*

The guidelines published by the Board of Parole list the "customary time" convicts should serve for particular crimes. For prisoners with good behavior and "very good parole prognosis," theft of less than $1,000—6 to 10 months; possession of marijuana—8 to 10 months; passing counterfeit money—12 to 16 months; embezzlement of less than $20,000—12 to 16 months; theft, forgery, or fraud involving $20,000 to $100,000—16 to 20 months; sale of drugs—26 to 36 months. For some crimes, the average time served by prisoners turned out to be a good bit higher than the Board of Parole's "customary total time." Customary time for a burglary was listed at 16 to 20 months, while the average time served by prisoners released the previous year was 33.7 months. Customary time for robbery was listed at 26 to 36 months, while the average time served was 53.7 months.[3]

"Parole prognosis," according to the guidelines, would be

determined by a "salient factor" score. Prior convictions, a history of drug use, use of a stolen car to commit the crime, and whether the prisoner completed high school were among the salient factors that figured in the Board of Parole's decisions.

Nearly 90 percent of the people behind bars are in state prisons. For the most part, they do not have the advantage Federal prisoners now enjoy of being able to consult published guidelines of parole criteria. The Federal guidelines may be vague. In some cases they seem absurd (for example, longer customary time for possession of marijuana than for theft). Some of the salient factors would produce class and race discrimination (for example, the weight given completion of high school). But the very existence of the guidelines limits the arbitrariness of decision making and gives prisoners some clues for assessing their chances for parole.

New York State has no published criteria. The Citizens' Inquiry on Parole and Criminal Justice recently had an opportunity to observe parole hearings in New York and discerned some operating guidelines. What follows is taken from their report.[4]

The New York Parole Board is primarily interested in whether a prisoner has been rehabilitated, or is "ready" for parole. Rehabilitation is measured by:

1. The inmate's psychological condition. "The board expects the inmate to claim that he has 'gained new insight into himself' while in the institution," the Citizens' Inquiry reports.

The board is favorably influenced if the inmate has good reports from a psychiatrist or psychologist he has seen regularly [5] or from a discussion leader of a group therapy program in which he has participated. If he has refused therapy and the board believes he needs it, or if the reports are unfavorable, the inmate's chances for parole are considerably lessened. The prisoner is expected to attribute his psychological development to one or more of the prison's programs or to the experience of incarceration.

If the prisoner insists he is innocent and does not show remorse, it is considered a very serious mark against him.

2. The prisoner's past criminal record, and whether his criminal behavior derived from alcoholism or drug addiction.

3. The prisoner's behavior in prison. The Citizens' Inquiry says that "the board uses the granting of parole as a device for controlling inmate behavior during incarceration." Participation in prison programs sponsored by organizations such as the Dale Carnegie Institute, the Jaycees, and the Toastmasters would be helpful to a prisoner.

4. The prisoner's behavior during any previous period of probation or parole.

5. The prisoner's parole plans. The board wants to know whether he will return to his wife, live with his parents, enroll in a drug program, or move to another community.

To implement these "standards," the twelve-member New York Parole Board divides itself into three-member panels. A panel visits each prison in the state once a month. Prisoners appear before these panels for periods ranging from about three minutes to as long as ten minutes. They are asked a series of stock questions.

The most common are:

Why did you commit the crime?
How did you feel about it at the time?
How do you feel about it now?
Would you do it again?
How have you adjusted here?
What have you learned while you have been "doing time"?
How is your family?
Do you write to your wife?
Does she write to you?
Do you miss your children?
You have been in trouble with the law for a long time, when are you going to change?

If we release you this time, do you think you can "make it" out on the street?

What are your plans if you are paroled?

How will you treat your parole officer?

Will you talk with him if you have any problems?

Do you think you are ready to live a good, clean, law-abiding life?

Are you willing to work?

Have you learned your lesson? [6]

William R. Coons was sentenced to three years in Attica prison for possession of LSD. Coons, a college English instructor, kept a diary of his prison experiences. He describes his interview with the New York Parole Board:

"Just answer the questions Yes or No, answer all questions, please. Did you sell drugs?"

"I pleaded guilty to the charge of Possession of a Dangerous Drug. The sale—"

"Just Yes or No, please. Did you sell drugs?"

"In my estimation there was no legitimate—"

"We're not asking you about that. We want to know if there was an agent, and you gave him something, and he gave you some money in return. Yes or no."

"Yes."

"Have you used drugs?"

"Yes." Short, and simple, let's get out of here. F. Lee Bailey couldn't do a thing with this. It's murder. "LSD, marijuana, hashish."

"Hmm. What started you on drugs?"

"Well, I went to see this ear, nose and throat specialist on Long Island seven or eight years ago. I had a persistent bronchial complaint, upper respiratory infections, the like. Anyway, he put me on these pills called Daprycyl. Which I later found out were a combination of dextroamphetamine, phenobarbital, and aspirin."

"Goofballs," the Spanish-looking guy on the right, a recent appointee, says. The one in the middle remains silent and is invisible except for the gleam of his glasses. He may be God.

"Well, and how long did you take these—goofballs—Mr. Coons?"

"I had a reusable prescription which I kept going for two years. I was pretty sick after that and started to get into the other stuff for relief."

Back to the Admiral. "Well, Mr. Coons, do you believe all this—incarceration—was really necessary?"

It's such an unbelievable question I don't answer. I just blink at him, stunned. Was he really asking me that? Some faint sense of embarrassment for him made me squirm in my seat.

He let it ride but soon got tough again. He bawled me out, his partner tossed in some remarks about possible sexual deviation (some ex-girlfriend must have squealed) just to let me know they had a lot more in their dossier than they needed to show, enough to keep me in jail for life, in fact, and then it was all over and I said "Thank you" and left.[7]

Perhaps the worst response a prisoner could give to any of these questions would be to insist he was innocent of the crime for which he was convicted. This would demonstrate to the parole board the prisoner had no remorse, had learned no lesson, and might do it again (despite his protestations that he never did it in the first place). " 'No confession, no parole,' " George Jackson wrote to Fay Stender, his lawyer, in one of his letters from Soledad Prison. "No one walks into the board room with his head up. This just isn't done! Guys lie to each other, but if a man gets a parole from these prisons, Fay, it means that he crawled into that room." [8]

The board that is supposed to make intelligent judgments on the basis of a prisoner's hurried and self-serving answers to its questions comprises both people who have worked their way up through the professional staff of the state prison system and political appointees. Among the latter, the New York board in 1973 included three former sheriffs and a former assistant appointments secretary to then Governor Nelson Rockefeller. No special training or education is required for service on the board. The salaries are over $32,000 a year, and the chairman gets over $38,000.

Besides the interview, a parole board member's only other source of information about a prisoner is the case file. These files are prepared hastily and carelessly. The prisoner has no right to see his own file, so he never has a chance to try to correct errors. Only one member of the three-person panel reads the case file, and he sees it just a few minutes before the inmate appears for the interview. All three members of the panel must approve parole if it is to be granted.

When a prisoner is turned down for parole, no reasons need be given. Occasionally a prisoner learns the reasons during his interview with the parole board.

I can't believe that my parole was denied for another year [an Indiana prisoner wrote to his parents]. Everybody here told me I was going to be paroled, I was stunned when Mr. Rudikell [the parole board chairman] denied me. He was furious with me for not having gone to school and for not having learned a trade. I told him I had a high school education, had my own auto mechanic shop outside (or did have once) and had worked as a master mechanic for 10 years. He said working as a mechanic was how I met bad companions and got in trouble. He said that due to the foreclosure proceedings against me, I would no longer be permitted to work as an auto mechanic. What will I do?

Mr. Rudikell said it was obvious that I was financially irresponsible. He had a transcript of the foreclosure and wouldn't hear my explanation that the foreclosure squared all my creditor accounts. He was quite disturbed, he said that I was misleading you and mother. (What did he mean by that?) He also said I was being denied parole because of the nature of my crime [burglary]. Said I should join some hobby clubs in here. Another board member recommended that I join Alcoholics Anonymous and attend meetings regularly, and when I reminded him that I didn't have a drinking problem, he said it was obvious that I wasn't interested in solving my character problems.[9]

Most prisoners are left to guess why they are going to spend an additional year behind bars, or however long it takes until they are again eligible for parole. The next panel to consider a prisoner for parole is also left in the dark about the earlier panel's reasons for turning down the prisoner.

A prisoner has no right to the assistance of counsel when he faces a parole board. If the board, in its sole and unexplained discretion, turns down a prisoner's application, the prisoner has no right of appeal to higher authority or the courts.

Special factors may override a parole board's usual criteria. If the crime got a lot of publicity, a parole board will treat the prisoner more harshly so it won't be accused of leniency. Parole boards also get information on crimes a prisoner is said to have committed, even though he was never convicted or even charged with the crime. As in the case of crimes enumerated in pre-sentence reports given to judges, a prisoner has no access to this information and no opportunity to defend himself against such allegations. Jessica Mitford says it is a frequent practice in California for a "frustrated D.A., unable to secure a conviction, [to get] his man in the end anyway" [10] by a letter to the Adult Authority.

The Adult Authority in California is even more powerful than parole boards elsewhere. It controls sentencing in California. As James V. Bennett describes it,

The judges decided only whether men were to be sent to prison or placed on probation. Not until six months after the commitment of prisoners did the real sentencing procedure begin. During these months, the men underwent diagnostic testing by trained personnel and the caseworkers had time to gather personal information that cast light on the cases. The Adult Authority reviewed this evidence, granted the men initial hearings, and set the dates on which they would be considered for parole. In effect, the Authority measured the men's progress in prison and examined their "release plans"—home, employment, supervision required, and so on. Then the Authority decided whether to grant parole or not.[11]

Bennett, a humane man, says he proposed duplication of the California scheme on the Federal level. His proposal was shot down, he says, "because many federal judges feared any form of adult authority program as an encroachment upon their prerogatives." [12] Apparently, the inhumane features of the California system, not discussed by Bennett, played no part   the failure to get the system adopted by the Federal government.

The inhumane part of the California system stems from the Adult Authority's power to defer fixing a parole date. When the prisoner appears before the Authority six months after he has been sent to prison, he can simply be told to come back the next year to get a parole date fixed. This can, and does, go on year after year. The prisoner never knows how long he has to serve. The agony is not so exquisite as not knowing the reasons for a sentence. It is the far greater agony of never knowing the length of a sentence.

Norval Morris recommends something like the California system, minus the deferral of decisions about the parole date. The prisoner would spend a brief period at a reception and diagnostic center and then go before the parole board to get his release date fixed. Morris would give the prison power to maintain discipline by allowing the cancellation of "good time" if the prisoner misbehaved. The misbehavior would have to be proved at a disciplinary hearing. The "good time" forfeited would be a defined and relatively short period.

Morris offers two principal arguments for his system. First, it is better practical politics than complete elimination of parole. "Change," he says, "can be facilitated by preserving vocational opportunities for those currently involved in the penal system. Prison, like other social institutions, serves its functionaries." [13] Morris's plan would fix sentences early while preserving jobs for parole boards and their staffs. His other argument is that it would allow "the determination of the period to be served at a time removed from the emotional intensity of a criminal trial." [14]

I can't quarrel with Morris's realpolitik. Unquestionably, it would be easier to achieve early fixing of sentences if it could be done without threatening the many jobs dependent on dragging out the process. My objection to his plan is rooted in Morris's other argument in favor of it.

When Morris tells us sentencing by a parole board is "removed from the emotional intensity of a criminal trial," he is also saying it will be done without public scrutiny. This would exacerbate the lawlessness of sentencing. I believe we should go in exactly the opposite direction. Judges should impose fixed terms. This would make judges, not parole boards, responsible for the time people spend in prison. They should explain their sentences to allow appellate review. This would reduce disparities.

Appellate review also addresses the problem of the "emotional intensity" of a trial. An appellate court wouldn't face the aggrieved victim, and its decision making would be a bit removed from the glare of publicity that sometimes surrounds trials. But its decision would be out in the open, with articulated reasons reconciling the punishment meted out to a particular defendant with previous punishments in similar circumstances. By its nature, a parole board's decisions are secretive. The reasons are not explained, and no appeal is possible when a wrong is done.

Morris attaches little importance to the brief period he would confine a prisoner in a reception and diagnostic center as an indicator of the appropriate date for parole. "Thirty years of careful compilation of base expectancy rates for parole revocation risk and later conviction risk," says Morris, "reveal that only three possible changes in the life of the prisoner during his incarceration are correlated with his later conformity to the conditions of his parole and with his avoidance of conviction for crime after his release—the availability of a family or other supportive social group for him to join on release; the availability of a reasonably supportive job; and the process and duration of aging itself." [15] A sentencing judge can estimate the effects of these as well as a parole board that meets a short period after the start of a prison sentence.

The reception and diagnostic center's primary purpose, in Morris's scheme, would be to arrange "an educational, training, or treatment program relating available services to the prisoner's felt needs." This would be done *after* the parole date was set, and would play no part in determining the date for release. I subscribe to Morris's view of the role that should be played by such diagnostic centers, only arguing that in fairness to convicts and everyone else, the sentencing process should be visible, explained, and appealable. This means that it should be in court.

There are two possible justifications for parole. First, parole would be justified if the people making the decisions to release people into the community could predict who would go back to crime. Second, it could be justified if the conditions of parole itself reduced such repetition of criminal behavior. Neither justification has support in the studies conducted to date.

"There is no empirical evidence to support the assertion that professional correctional workers, even when supplied with full case histories, can assess the probability of prisoners' success on parole," say Ronald Goldfarb and Linda Singer.[16] They review the scholarly literature on the subject. It is unanimous in flunking the parole prediction. The comprehensive study by the Citizens' Inquiry on Parole and Criminal Justice reached a similar conclusion. The Citizens' Inquiry also found "no statistical evidence demonstrating that the social service [New York] provides to parolees reduces recidivism. And the commission's interviews with parolees and the research conducted in other jurisdictions strongly suggest that the present social services are ineffective in reducing recidivism." [17]

As in the case of probation, parole has some utility as a low-level punishment. There should be no barrier to a judge's sentencing a person to a period in prison followed by a period with the lesser restriction of parole. The appropriateness of parole as part of a punishment scheme could be known at sentencing. The only reason for deferring judgment would be if it could be shown that deferral increased knowledge about recidivism. Since this cannot be shown, the only fair way to use parole is to build it into the original sentencing process. (Probation would then be the proper name for it.) Putting aside Morris's warnings about the difficulties of doing away with the jobs, I am for eliminating the present form of post-sentencing parole along with parole boards and their staffs.

If parole is to be used as a low-level punishment, the conditions ought to be different from those now prevalent. These are a few of the conditions of parole in New York State:

He hereby consents to any search of his person, his residence, or any property or premises under his control which the Board of Parole or any of its representatives may see fit to make at any time in their discretion.

... must not associate with evil companions ... support his dependents, if any, and assume toward them all legal and moral obligations.

He must avoid the excessive use of intoxicating beverages and abstain completely if so directed by his parole officer.

He must not live as man and wife with anyone to whom he is not legally married and will consult with his parole officer before he applies for a license to marry.

Immediately after his release on parole he must surrender any motor vehicle license which he had in his possession ... must not carry from the institution from which he is released, or send to any penal institution ... any written or verbal messages.

... must not register as a voter and must not vote.

And so it goes. Violation of any of these rules is grounds for revocation of parole.

The standards I envision for probation/parole would include regular reporting to a parole officer or other public official and the performance of public-service work, perhaps over and above any other job held by the person. These would be low-level punishments, but they would not be as demeaning or as absurdly Victorian as the rules now in force. It cannot be useful to engender the cynicism and deceptions in parolees that must result from present-day rules.

As it presently operates, parole serves a couple of useful purposes. It mitigates the harshness of some criminal sentences. My proposal to eliminate parole assumes a rational sentencing structure. In the absence of sensible sentences, I would still want parole as a way of releasing early from prison people who might otherwise serve five or ten years behind bars for property crimes.

Parole and its cousin "good time" also serve prison-management purposes. I favor a very limited flexibility in sentences to allow wardens to maintain disciplinary control over inmates. The Committee on the Study of Incarceration, which supports elimination of parole, suggests that up to 5 percent of a prisoner's sentence could be conditional on good behavior. Another group anxious to get rid of parole, the American Friends Service Committee, suggests similarly limited flexibility. "Some small proportion of the punishment," they write, "may be left variable in order to reward conformity to rules during periods of punishment and thereby reduce social control problems in prisons." But "it must be recognized," the Friends group caution, "that when good time is regularly given, failure to grant good time is itself the delivery of a penal sanction. Therefore it is a judicial matter and the accused prisoner should enjoy the safeguards of due process." [18]

Opposition to parole is mounting. It has been a principal target of inmate fury in all of the prison riots of the last several years. Parole was high on the list of grievances of the prisoners at Attica, and one of the reform proposals accepted by New York State (before the negotiations broke down and the shooting started) demonstrates some of the absurdity of parole. "Paroled inmates," the state temporarily agreed, "shall not be charged with parole violations for moving traffic violations or driving without a license, unconnected with any other crime." The New York State commission that investigated the Attica riot found that "Inmates' criticisms were echoed by many parole officers and corrections personnel, who agreed that the operation of the parole system was a primary source of tension and bitterness within the walls." [19] The irony here is that the principal management device of prison officials was a main factor in making prison management impossible.

In May 1975, fifteen prisoners in New York State filed suit, challenging the constitutionality of New York's parole system. The suit, the first of its kind, was brought for the prisoners by the New York Civil Liberties Union. It argues that the state's parole law "vests the parole board with standardless and unfettered discretion" in violation of the United States Constitution's guarantee of due process of law. Another way of putting the problem is the way it is stated by the chairman of the United States Board of Parole, Maurice Sigler. As he sees it, "We have this terrible power. We sit up here playing God."

16
Stigma

Alvin Lake was arrested for robbery. It was not his first contact with the police and the courts. When he was fifteen, his mother had him arrested as an incorrigible child. He spent six months in a state training school before running away to live with his grandmother. Nobody ever came to pick him up from his grandmother's house.

The robbery arrest came when he was nineteen. He was caught holding up a liquor store. The police decided Lake (not his real name) was the man they wanted for a string of shop burglaries in the area. He said it wasn't so, that they were just trying to clear their case loads. The prosecutor believed the police. Perhaps the defense lawyer also thought Lake had committed all the burglaries in addition to robbery of the liquor store. Between them, the two lawyers concluded a fairly harsh bargain for a first arrest for robbery. Lake went to prison for five years. He didn't make parole and, with time off for good behavior, left prison after nearly four years behind bars.

When Lake got out, he applied for a license to practice the trade he had learned inside the prison: barbering. Sorry, he was told, ex-convicts can't be licensed as barbers. Lake thought he would like to try construction work. No go. The apprenticeship program wouldn't accept him because of his criminal record. Lake had talent. He could play the piano and sing. Perhaps he could entertain in a bar. He stopped by a tavern and was told he would

201

need a cabaret license before they would consider him. Again, the same story: No cabaret license if you are an ex-convict. Lake went back to the tavern because the owner had seemed fairly pleasant. Could he do any work at all around the place? Perhaps sweep up? Yes, that might be possible. But first, since he was an ex-convict, he would need the permission of the state alcohol-control agency. Of course, they were fairly slow. It might take months until they gave permission. And they might not give permission. Since his crime was against a liquor store, the agency might very well turn Lake down as a tavern employee.

Lake finally got a job. He became a dishwasher in a cafeteria. At the place on the job application form where it asked about any criminal record, he lied. He said he had never been convicted or even arrested. Twenty-nine days later, Lake was fired. His employer had found out about Lake's conviction for robbery. He wasn't fired for that, according to the man who had hired him. He was fired because he had lied about the conviction on his employment application form. After thirty days on the job, Lake would have become a union member. The union would have been able to contest his dismissal, possibly even taking it to arbitration. On the day he was fired, Lake was still a probationary employee and could be fired at the discretion of his employer.

Lake told this story in a letter to me from Attica prison. He was there for another robbery, just four months after he got out the time before. The next time he gets out, he won't have much hope of doing better. If people don't want convicted robbers around, they are even less likely to want to hire someone convicted a second time.

Millions of people are denied jobs and licenses because of criminal records. Arrest records not followed by convictions are often equally damaging.

Brian Naylor (also a made-up name) was arrested for a crime similar to Alvin Lake's. A police car picked him up because he fit the description of a man who had held up a gas station in the neighborhood just a few minutes earlier. Naylor, who was seventeen at the time, was taken to the police station, booked, and fingerprinted. Four hours later, he was released. The gas station owner saw Naylor in a lineup and told the police they had arrested the wrong person. But Naylor's arrest record got around, and he had as much trouble as Alvin Lake in getting a job. The presumption of innocence, the most important tenet of our system of criminal justice, did not protect him against punishment by arrest-record dissemination. Two years later, he was arrested for burglary. This time, Naylor was convicted.

In another book, *Dossier: The Secret Files They Keep on You,*[1] I described the ways arrest-and-conviction records circulate and the damage they do to people. Collected and disseminated in the belief that this is a way of fighting crime, the records turn out to have very little use in apprehending criminals. Instead, they create much of the problem they are supposed to solve. People are stigmatized by their records and excluded by them from society's mainstream. They are denied the stabilizing influence of steady homes and jobs and are forced into crime. The records virtually guarantee a repeat performance in people like Alvin Lake and may start someone like Brian Naylor on a life of crime.

The pages that follow are a postscript to *Dossier.* In the year or so since *Dossier* was published, Congress has done nothing to control the distribution of arrest-and-conviction records. The principal congressional champion of limits, Senator Sam Ervin, has retired to the hills and streams of North Carolina. No one has emerged to take his place on Capitol Hill as a comparably forceful and effective champion of privacy.

One of Ervin's legacies was the Privacy Act of 1974. To get it adopted, he had to agree to exclude law-enforcement records from its provisions, giving citizens access to information about them in Federal data banks. Ervin fought until his last days in office to get Congress to approve a Senate bill limiting the circulation of arrest-and-conviction records. For a brief period, it looked as though he would succeed. His efforts were finally defeated by an unusual coalition. Despite President Ford's pledge when he took office that his administration would give "hot pursuit [to] tough laws" to protect privacy, the bill was opposed by the Department of Justice. In deference to the stand of the Ford administration, Senator Roman Hruska, senior Republican on Ervin's Subcommittee on Constitutional Rights, backed away from a compromise bill he had hammered out with Ervin. The other partner in the coalition opposed to limiting circulation of arrest-and-conviction records was a segment of the press led by the Reporters Committee for Freedom of the Press.

The Reporters Committee is a newly organized group numbering some of America's best journalists among its members. Its principal organizer and spokesman is Jack Landau, a reporter for the Newhouse newspapers, noted for the zeal he devotes to the cause he is serving at the moment. A onetime aide to then Attorney General John Mitchell, he was briefly among the most enthusiastic champions of Mitchell's stewardship of the Department of Justice. Mitchell, in turn, entrusted Landau with one of the most nefarious adventures of.the Nixon years, a secret visit to two Justices of the United States Supreme Court in an unsuccessful effort to persuade them to reverse their decisions in a case because of its impact on "national security." Later, as an organizer of the Reporters Committee, Landau became a zealous opponent of Nixon administration assaults on press freedom.

For reasons I find unfathomable, Landau decided that legislative proposals and court decisions to protect the privacy of records are among the great threats to freedom of the press. Senator Ervin's bill would have barred the use of arrest-and-conviction records except by law-enforcement agencies for law-enforcement purposes. Landau and some of his colleagues want free access by the press to all such records. There are no stronger arguments for this position than for giving the press access to income-tax records, medical records of persons treated in public hospitals, individually identifiable files gathered by the Census Bureau, case files of people getting public welfare, personnel employment files of public employees, or many other kinds of records gathered by the government. All these dossiers would damage private persons if revealed. Still, raising the question of press access gave some opponents of limits on arrest-record dissemination a principled reason they had previously lacked to oppose Ervin's legislation.

Congressional proposals to deal with the problem were considered again in 1975 with John Tunney as the principal sponsor of controls on arrest records in the Senate and Don Edwards as the leading advocate in the House of Representatives. The Department of Justice continued to oppose the legislation. At a July 1975 hearing, Deputy Attorney General Harold R. Tyler, Jr., informed a Senate committee that legislation on arrest records was "premature." The FBI has been collecting and disseminating these records since 1924, has a staff of several thousand people who disseminate millions of records annually to licensing agencies and employers, and is now experimenting with satellite transmission of arrest records to ensure they follow people even more efficiently. Still, the Department of Justice thinks legislation to control all this is premature! And because there is not much of an organized lobby on the other side and Congress has nobody who fills the vacuum left by Ervin, it will possibly be some time yet before Federal legislation is adopted.

There is more progress in the state legislatures. The Connecticut legislature overrode a veto by then Governor Thomas Meskill in 1974 and authorized expungement of arrest records not followed by convictions. Florida, Hawaii, Illinois, Maine, and Massachusetts all have some legislation limiting circulation or use of arrest records. New York adopted sweeping legislation in 1975 authorizing expungement of all arrest records not resulting in convictions, and barring employment discrimination against people with such records, but it was vetoed by Governor Hugh Carey. He said he was generally in favor of such a law, but the bill before him did not suit him. At the same time, Carey also vetoed an omnibus repeal of postconviction employment disabilities.

State legislation in this area, of course, does not reach the FBI. The Bureau continues to disseminate arrest records to employers in states that have legislated against circulating the records. Although some members of Congress, such as Senator Strom Thurmond, profess opposition to Federal arrest-records legislation because it restricts states' rights, in practice the Federal government now overrides state legislation attempting to protect privacy.

The courts have made a little headway in dealing with arrest-and-conviction records. In October 1974, the United States Court of Appeals for the District of Columbia Circuit decided *Tarlton* v. *Saxbe*, a case brought by a convict who said that incomplete and inaccurate information in his FBI file had hurt him at sentencing and in the decision of a parole board to deny him parole. The court decision required "such reasonable care as the F.B.I. is able to afford to avoid injury to innocent citizens through dissemination of inaccurate information."

In March 1975, the Superior Court of the District of Columbia considered a challenge to record expungement in which the assertion was made that it is an improper rewriting of history. "It is clear," the court said in *U.S.* v. *Hudson*, that "when policy requires, our system of law renders existing documents and transactions null and void, permits the denial of facts, and adopts presumptions and legal fictions."

And, in June 1975, the FBI consented for the first time to the expungement of the record of a legal arrest made by the Bureau. The action came in the face of a lawsuit by "Jane Doe," a prominent educator who had been arrested more than two decades earlier when she was a young girl and newly married to a man who had concealed his criminal life from her. She was arrested with her husband for transporting stolen property across state lines, but the charges against her were dropped when law-enforcement officials realized she was more a victim of her husband than an accomplice. Jane Doe had her marriage annulled and went on to college and graduate education and, over a period of time, built a new life and a distinguished career. She passed up several opportunities for advancement, however, for fear they would provide occasions for revelation of her youthful arrest record. The expungement of her arrest record lifted a weight from her shoulders and set a precedent.

By mid-1976, the United States Supreme Court will decide

Davis v. *Paul,* a case with very important implications for people with arrest records that did not result in convictions. Edward Charles Davis, III, a photographer for the *Louisville Courier-Journal,* was arrested in Louisville, Kentucky, on a charge of shoplifting. The arrest was apparently a mistake, and the charges against Davis were dismissed. Even so, the Louisville and Jefferson County police departments included Davis's name and photograph in a flyer captioned "Active Shoplifters." The flyer was distributed to merchants in the Louisville metropolitan area shortly before Christmas 1972 to alert them "to watch for these subjects."

"In the case at bar," the United States Court of Appeals for the Sixth Circuit decided, Davis

alleges that he and others have been branded as active shoplifters—common criminals—and grouped together with those who have been convicted of crimes. This label carries with it the badge of disgrace of a criminal conviction. Moreover, it is a direct statement by law enforcement officials that the persons included in the flyer are presently pursuing an active course of criminal conduct. All this was done without the slightest regard for due process. There was no notice nor opportunity to refute the charges in a criminal proceeding. It goes without saying that the Police Chiefs cannot determine the guilt or innocence of an accused man in an administrative proceeding. Such a determination can be made only in a court of law.

The harm is all the more apparent because the branding has been done by law enforcement officials with the full power, prestige, and authority of their positions. There can be little doubt that a person's standing and associations in the community have been damaged seriously when law enforcement officials brand him an active shoplifter, accuse him of a continuing course of criminal conduct, group him with criminals and distribute his name and photograph to the merchants and business people of the community. Such acts are a direct and devastating attack on the good name, reputation, honor and integrity of the person involved. The fact of an arrest without more may impair or cloud a person's reputation.

If the Supreme Court agrees with the lower court, it will open law-enforcement officials to suits for money damages if they distribute records of arrests not followed by convictions to non-law-enforcement agencies. The *Davis* case could become a landmark in protecting the presumption of innocence for people not convicted of crimes.

Courts and state legislatures have also been making some progress in lifting the statutory disabilities imposed on people with conviction records. In the last couple of years, more than a dozen states have adopted laws eliminating some or all specific prohibitions on licensing ex-convicts to hold certain jobs or on allowing ex-convicts to work for state and local governments. This does not mean that a lot of ex-convicts are getting government jobs or jobs in licensed occupations. They must still contend with discrimination against people with criminal records. It only means the discrimination is no longer absolutely mandated by state law in those jurisdictions which have repealed prohibitions on licensing or public employment for ex-convicts.

Court decisions overturning licensing or public-employment restrictions on ex-convicts are still relatively rare. One of the more significant rulings was by a three-judge Federal court in the case of Chester Harris, a master barber in Kentucky from 1958 until 1970. Harris was convicted of the sale of narcotics in 1970 and was sentenced to five years in prison. In 1973, he was released on parole. When he got out of prison, Harris was no longer allowed to practice his profession. His license had been revoked while he was in prison because of his felony conviction. "We are unable to perceive the rational connection between the plaintiff's fitness to practice barbering and the statute which has an across-the-board disqualification based on his having been convicted of any felony," said the three Federal judges in finding unconstitutional the statute under which Harris's license was revoked.

As yet, only a relative handful of the people disabled by arrest-and-conviction records have benefited from actions by legislatures and courts to remove from them the stigmas and disabilities caused by their records. Were it not that many people get away with lies about their past records, even greater numbers would be unemployable and, therefore, probably living off crime. Dishonesty about past records is the most effective contemporary mechanism for rehabilitation. But some people are honest about their records. Many more don't get away with lies because too many government agencies and private businesses are dedicated to ferreting out the truth and preventing people with criminal records from escaping their stigma.

The handicaps of criminal records imposed on millions of people are, I believe, among the major causes of crime in the United States. These handicaps are created by government. Government disseminates the records and adopts the laws and rules denying government jobs and licenses to hold private jobs to people with criminal records. Government can undo the harm it creates by halting the dissemination of records and repealing the laws imposing employment disabilities on people with records.

Britain has recently taken a major step in this direction, even though the problem was never so serious in that country as in the United States. Arrest records not resulting in convictions are not routinely maintained by law-enforcement agencies in Britain and are almost never disseminated. Conviction records are maintained and do circulate, though without the efficiency achieved by the FBI and the American credit-reporting industry. Despite the much smaller significance of the criminal-record stigma in Britain (or, perhaps, because it has a less significant problem, Britain has fewer people with a vested interest in the maintenance of the problem), Parliament adopted new legislation in 1975 sealing records of all persons who were sentenced up to thirty months in prison, providing they avoided subsequent conviction. Since criminal sentences in Britain are very much lower than in the United States, the thirty-month ceiling affects a substantial majority of the ex-convict population. A million people—not very many by United States standards, but Britain has much less crime than we have—were allowed to begin over again with a clean slate. A few categories of employment, including lawyers, doctors, police, and prison officers, were exempted from new rules prohibiting employment discrimination against ex-convicts. The government rejected requests for exemptions by bankers, diamond and gold merchants, securities dealers, and customs authorities.

If exemptions from rules against discrimination are allowed, there may be a better way to devise them than has been adopted by the British. Rather than exempt specific occupations, I would allow discrimination based on past convictions for serious crimes directly relevant to a particular occupation. An applicant for a job as a school janitor could be turned down on the basis of a past conviction for child molestation or arson, but not for robbery. A would-be bank clerk could be rejected on the basis of a conviction for embezzlement and robbery, but not for child molestation. A regulatory agency in the system I envision would establish procedures for determining what inquiries are appropriate for particular categories of employment.

It will be extremely difficult to secure such legislation in the United States. Crime is so pervasive in our country and our fear of it so great that we feel we cannot afford remedies that might mitigate the problem of crime in the nation while increasing the immediate dangers we face in our daily lives. People can accept the proposition that there will be less crime if ex-convicts can get jobs, but they don't want ex-convicts working and living alongside them.

A Puritan legacy perceiving stigma as part of the punishment for wrongdoing is also a factor in the American reluctance to deal with the problem of criminal records. This is also true of arrest records that result in dismissals and acquittals and prove no wrongdoing. Law-enforcement publicists have persuaded most people that "technicalities" and "lawyers' tricks" are the reasons for most failures to convict people. Arrest records, at least where they are other people's arrest records,[2] are generally regarded as indications of probable guilt.

We pay a stiff penalty in crime for our insistence on continuing to stigmatize people with arrest-and-conviction records. The people who opt for private safety and hope to get it by discrimination against people with criminal records only achieve the safety they seek—if then—if they carefully insulate all parts of their lives from exposure to criminals. With so many criminals around, many living criminal lives because their stigmas deny them alternatives, it is very difficult to secure complete prophylactic protection. As for the Puritan ethic of punishing wrongdoing, it punishes the victims of people confined to criminal lives as effectively as it punishes the criminals.

17
Summing Up

"A wise and frugal government," Thomas Jefferson said in his first inaugural address, "shall restrain men from injuring one another." Except for this essential task, Jefferson believed government should "leave them otherwise free to regulate their own pursuits." The repeal of laws against public drunkenness, consensual sexual acts, drug possession, and status offenses would move us in the direction of the Jeffersonian ideal. It would also cut in half the total number of arrests nationwide. Police, prosecutors, and courts could concentrate on the violent crimes—murder, rape, robbery, and aggravated assault—presently comprising only about 4 percent of all arrests, and such property crimes as burglary, larceny, and vandalism. Their present preoccupation with crimes that do not injure others reduces our police to the role of the sacred geese on the grounds of the Capitol in ancient Rome. They can cackle about thieves in the night but can do them no harm.

The preceding pages have not dealt with such victimless crimes as vagrancy, loitering, obscenity, and gambling because they are of declining significance as a diversion of police energies from more serious matters. To the extent that vagrancy and loitering laws represent something beyond supplemental powers to use against public drunkenness and prostitution, they are being held unconstitutional by the courts. And although the Burger

212

Supreme Court has upheld the constitutionality of obscenity prosecutions, law-enforcement officials in much of the country are giving up their efforts to shield Americans from sexually explicit books, movies, and magazines. In part, this reflects a maturation of public opinion about obscenity, making it difficult to get juries to convict people charged with selling or producing the materials. The decline is also attributable to the development of a highly specialized segment of the legal profession. It gives the pornography industry very skillful and usually successful representation in the courts. In return, the lawyers earn handsome fees. The difficulty in obtaining convictions has made prosecutors in many communities discourage police from spending a great deal of their time on obscenity.

Gambling laws still consume a substantial amount of police effort, but enforcement is sporadic. The New York City police, for example, no longer pay much attention to the numbers business. Perhaps this is because the police recognize the anomaly of arresting some people for a form of gambling very similar to the governmentally sponsored and promoted lotteries and off-track betting now flourishing alongside the numbers business. Then, too, the numbers business now seems to treat its customers fairly well. It gives better odds than the New York State Lottery and pays winners promptly and fully. The numbers business in New York can no longer even be said to be siphoning money from the city's black population since the principal entrepreneurs deriving profit from it and their employees are now black. It is one of New York's more successful ventures in black capitalism.

The gambling laws are enforced these days either as a means of prosecuting people in organized crime against whom other charges are more difficult to prove or as a way of appeasing communities outraged by fairly open violation of the laws. Since not so many people are outraged anymore, arrests and prosecutions are diminishing in numbers. The FBI estimates that there were 93,300 arrests for gambling in 1971 and that the number had declined to 68,300 in 1973, a decrease of 27 percent in just two years. When the gambling laws are enforced, it often costs law enforcement a great deal of time and effort. In part, this is because gambling is the principal crime susceptible to prosecution through the accumulation of evidence derived from wiretaps. Because of the large amount of time it takes to record, listen to, and transcribe tapes based on wiretapping, filled as they are with endless irrelevant conversations, wiretapping is extremely expensive.

The major use of wiretapping is in political surveillance. Additional saving of police energies could be achieved by dismantling the political-intelligence operations maintained by most law-enforcement agencies. The FBI recently revealed that $85 million of its $500-million-a-year budget goes for political surveillance. This is the Bureau's own estimate, probably understated, of the cost it incurs in such undertakings as its investigations of high school students who write to the Soviet embassy seeking information for term papers, its checks of the license plates of cars parked in the vicinity of meetings of radical political groups, and its photography of the participants in sundry demonstrations. Almost all local police departments of any size have their own "red squads" engaged in parallel activities. Proportionately, local police spend far less on political surveillance than the FBI. Even so, the combined cost is considerable (one can only guess at the total). Leaving aside the many other excellent reasons for terminating these efforts, it would certainly do a lot more good to have all the police now staffing "red squads" out driving patrol cars or investigating crimes of violence.

The victimless crimes focused on in this book are those continuing to occupy so much of the time available to the people we pay to protect us against crime that they cannot effectively do the job we need done. Whether the police could offer us much greater protection if they were not diverted by things that should be none of their business remains an open question. Certainly, no increase in the amount of time the police can devote to real crime would be of much use in dealing with the great number of murders, assaults, and rapes growing out of emotional relationships between people previously acquainted with each other.

These crimes are not susceptible to much action by the police beyond the fairly simple task of apprehending easily identifiable suspects. But what of other kinds of crime?

After reviewing various experiments in which greatly increased numbers of police were deployed in particular communities, a close student of the subject, Professor James Q. Wilson, finds it "hard to draw any comprehensive conclusions about the ability of the police to prevent crime that is not so guarded and cautious as to be useless."

But, Wilson goes on to observe, the suggestion seems warranted that "a massive increase in police presence on foot in densely settled areas will probably lead to a reduction in those crimes, such as muggings and auto theft, that require the perpetrators to use the city streets." The difficulty, says Wilson, is that "the cost of any massive increase is—well—massive." [1] Without disputing Wilson on the need to be cautious in making general statements about the impact additional police can make in preventing crime, it seems worth noting that we are already expending massively on the police. The General Accounting Office says that Federal government police activities cost $2.6 billion in fiscal 1975 and employed 169,625 persons. State and local governments probably spent close to $10 billion on law enforcement in the course of that year. Much of the money is being wasted. Too much police time is consumed by the wrong things.

Some will protest my categorization of prostitution, consensual sodomy, public drunkenness, drug possession, and PINS offenses as victimless crimes either because they believe it appropriate for the law to make it a crime to injure oneself or because—as in the case of prostitution—other crimes seem to be associated with the proscribed conduct. I do not dispute the injury people do themselves through such behaviors as public drunkenness or heroin use. I want to decriminalize these behaviors because I see no point in compounding the injury with legal punishment. The laws against such conduct victimize the people who engage in it far more than the conduct itself. As for the nexus between other crime and victimless crime, it, too, is largely a creation of the criminal law. Millions of people are criminally punished because of sexual practices increasingly accepted as normal; because their tastes in drugs include substances other than nicotine and alcohol; because they look unsightly; and, if they are children, because they have trouble with their parents or their schools. Pushed beyond the pale of the law, some of the people arrested on such charges begin to see themselves as they are seen by others: as criminals. It becomes just a bit easier for them to commit other crimes, perhaps crimes with victims.

Organized crime in America was largely created by Prohibition. The continuing prohibition approach to drugs, sex, and gambling has helped sustain it. By now, organized crime has mimicked other American business enterprises and diversified its operations. It is too well entrenched to disappear just because changes in the laws make it uneconomic to trade in heroin or cater to other forbidden tastes. But changes of that sort would diminish some of the financial rewards and thereby dim some of organized crime's attraction to new recruits.

A happy by-product of ending arrests for victimless crimes would be the great reduction in police abuse and corruption. Entrapment is not used against burglars. Dragnet arrests have no part in enforcing laws against rape or assault. American police have never been known to take payoffs from murderers. Wiretaps are not used against rapists. Victimless crimes bring out the worst in police, besides diverting their energies from more important things.

Corruption would also be reduced by bringing some people into police departments at command levels. Requiring every police officer to work his way up through the ranks ensures that those who go along with the venality around them are also those who obtain commands. Their earlier participation in corruption, or their silence when their fellow officers take bribes, diminishes their ability to act against corruption when they achieve command, even if they should be so inclined. They might as well relax and reconcile themselves to the fatter take that so often goes along with advancement in a police department.

The reduction in the number of arrests resulting from the elimination of victimless crimes would be a great help in ending plea bargaining. If it is not sufficient, and if more courtrooms, judges, and lawyers are needed, the cost seems well worth it. A rational criminal justice system cannot be constructed so long as the punishment for claiming innocence is often greater than for robbery and rape. An end to plea bargaining would also permit the machinery of justice to gain the dignity it so lacks today.

One of my proposals goes against the grain of the rest of the book. It would extend the reach of the criminal law. I would make all private ownership of guns illegal. In fact, if the citizenry could ever be disarmed—a very remote hope—the next step would be to strip police of their sidearms. I see not the slightest prospect of that coming to pass, but it would certainly mitigate their menace.

My proposal to prohibit all private ownership of guns is offered with considerable diffidence. Two centuries of stockpiled weapons argue against it. "About this gun control you have gotten yourself involved in," a man in Missouri wrote to me recently, "I think you should know that law-abiding people like me are not going to give up their guns no matter what kind of law would be passed." As in the case of a great many similar letters I received since I became known as a gun opponent, the letter concluded with a threat. Abandon this Communist conspiracy and "keep your dirty hands out of gun control issues," the man from Missouri advised me, else "the Day will come when you no longer exist."

The threats are probably not meant seriously—at least I hope they aren't serious. But gun owners are sincere in asserting they are "not going to give up their guns no matter what kind of law would be passed." My correspondent apparently saw no contradiction in describing himself as "law-abiding" and simultaneously professing resistance to any law against guns. It is an attitude shared by millions of other gun owners and cannot be overcome in our times. We should probably start by prohibiting all manufacture, import, or sale of guns and ammunition and by offering bounties to people who turn in their guns. Possession of guns should also be made illegal, but this means the law would be unenforceable or it would be enforced by unacceptable means. Neither is a good alternative.

I would revise our schemes for punishing people so as to put in prison for very long periods those who commit certain kinds of violent crime, those I have defined as "public crimes." For "private crimes" of violence and for property crimes, my proposals would reduce the length of prison sentences. The entire burden for determining the length of sentences would be taken away from parole boards. They would have no reason to exist. Punishment, I believe, should be determined in court by a judge after adversary proceedings according to standards fixed by legislatures. And it should be punishment, not rehabilitation.

The causes of crime, in my view, lie in the rootlessness, transiency, and lack of family cohesion that characterize American life. There is nothing novel in this view. It is consistent with the mainstream of social science thinking about crime. Even so, a web of public policy actively promotes the very rootlessness that does so much damage.

By reducing the number of arrests and by prohibiting most job discrimination against people with arrest-and-conviction records, my proposals would help keep families together. People would not have to go on the run to escape their records. I also propose to alter public policies that take children from their parents, split up parents, put children in juvenile jails for offenses not crimes when they are committed by adults, exclude children from school, shuttle children among foster homes, and deny children who need them permanent adoptive homes. Not all the children treated so shabbily end as criminals. But anyone in regular contact with people convicted of crimes soon discovers that the great majority did not have steady homes as children. Disruption of the lives of many children is inevitable and cannot be cured by public policy. But a very large part of the problem is created by the public policies I have identified. Even if they had no relationship to crime, they should be revised. Their part in causing crime adds urgency.

My unwillingness to deal with poverty and inequality as

causes of crime makes me susceptible to a charge of superficiality. My answer is that people have been poor and unequal in other times and other places without also becoming criminals. On the other hand, rootlessness and family disruption always seem to produce crime. When Englishmen flocked to London in the sixteenth and seventeenth centuries because of enclosure of the fields, and again at the end of the eighteenth century because of dislocation caused by the industrial revolution, they made it a very dangerous city. The frontier towns of the American West, brief homes for people moving on, were another notorious example of violence and thieving.

While many countries surpass us in poverty, and some in economic and racial inequality, we have no peer in the transiency of our lives. The United States of America is also the most crime-ridden nation on earth. I believe there is a cause-and-effect relationship.

I attribute much of our crime problem to public policies that tear families apart and send people on the run in search of opportunities where their records will not follow them. These policies exacerbate the rootlessness of American life. They can be revised in the short run without waiting for long-term solutions to poverty and racial inequality in America.

Elimination of criminal penalties for possession of marijuana seems a good possibility before the decade is out. Change here seems likely because of the shift in the demographic characteristics of the marijuana-using population. For the first time in the half century since the laws against it were enacted, marijuana is not particularly identified with a despised population. Betty Ford doesn't mind if people think the President's children have sampled marijuana. As long as the laws against the drug were primarily a weapon to use against Chicano immigrants to the Western states or against the more recent hippie culture, there was no possibility of repeal. But marijuana has long lost its identification with Chicanos, and the hippies have grown up and blended into the rest of the American population. Quondam hippies have acquired a taste for the comforts enjoyed by other Americans. In exchange, they have infected a lot of other people with some of their tastes in speech, clothing, hairstyles, and weeds. Now that marijuana users are becoming indistinguishable from everyone else, the days are numbered for the laws making its use a crime.

Heroin remains a drug used almost exclusively by hated people. Average Americans show no interest in it. There seems little likelihood we will emulate Britain's sane and sensible policies. The addict population in Britain is indistinguishable from everyone else and does not arouse the antagonism provoked by American "junkies."

Laws against public drunkenness, consensual sodomy, and prostitution are all useful in controlling populations average Americans find loathsome: derelicts, homosexual men (not homosexual women, who are not bothered), and dirty women who might infect men. Among these groups, homosexual men have been the most aggressive in asserting their own rights. By persuading reputable men to come out of the closet and by asserting a certain pride in being gay, they are mitigating the public's hostility to homosexuals. In another ten years or so, I expect, the laws against consensual homosexual behavior among adults will have disappeared.

Most of the other proposals I make lack constituencies capable of pressing for revision of public policy. The chances of their adoption seem fairly remote. The only predictable changes in the way we deal with crime are more of the same we have gotten in the last few years: increased police powers to use against people on the street after dark and against motorists, and technologically sophisticated identity checks.

With the help of the United States Supreme Court, police have transformed the state power to license motorists into a power to stop and search them. The wonders of computer technology make random stops an extremely valuable way of apprehending people wanted for crime, at least in the eyes of the law-enforcement community. The *Robinson* decision by the Supreme Court, following its earlier decisions in the "stop-and-frisk" cases, legitimizes random searches and makes the contraband discovered usable as evidence to prosecute people for crime. By degrees, and without any specific legislative awareness or action, the motor vehicle license is being made into the equivalent of the Soviet Union's internal passport.

These new police powers and identity checks produce several hundred thousand arrests annually. Occasionally, they also snare fugitives wanted for major crimes. But these are chance benefits. Many of the arrests have no purpose other than to legitimize random searches. As for the few real criminals caught by the computers, the price is too high. It is not worth the police intrusion into the lives of tens of millions of Americans any more than the seizure of some contraband would justify house-to-house searches of whole cities.

Nearly a decade ago, the President's Commission on Law Enforcement estimated a man's chance of being arrested at some time in his life at one in two. Since then, arrest rates have been climbing sharply. In part, this is because there is more crime. But not entirely. By far the steepest rise in arrest rates since the commission made its projections has been for the crime of marijuana possession. Serendipitous styles of law enforcement, combined with the maintenance of laws penalizing conduct that does not injure others, are creating a whole nation of people labeled as criminals. Fewer and fewer of us can qualify as the "average law-abiding citizens" for whose benefit J. Edgar Hoover and his successors have labored so diligently.

There is a passage in Thomas Mann's dark and brooding novel *Doctor Faustus* where the narrator pauses to comment on what is going on around him. It is early 1945 and Germany is being invaded. "It belongs in the realm of the fantastic," Mann has his narrator say, "it offends against all order and expectation that Germany itself should become the theater of one of Germany's wars." Similarly, it belongs in the realm of the fantastic and offends against all order and expectation that law-abiding citizens themselves shall become the theater of the FBI's war on crime. The Bureau and the local law-enforcement agencies it unites through the services of the National Crime Information Center and the Identification Division are stopping, searching, and arresting millions of Americans and disseminating records labeling them as criminals in a headlong rush to get as many opportunities as possible for chance "hits on the system." And just as Germany's fantastic adventure ended by devastating Germany, so the fantastic adventures of our law-enforcement apparatus are devastating our chances for living law-abiding lives.

Notes

PART ONE: CRIME

Chapter 1. The Crime of Sex

1. A 1973 Supreme Court decision, *United States* v. *Russell,* virtually eliminated a defendant's ability to avoid conviction by claiming entrapment.
2. Section 647(b) is the provision of California state law that prohibits soliciting or engaging in prostitution. Until 1961, it applied only to women. A revision at that time extended the *words* of the statute to cover males.

Chapter 2. Public Boozers

1. The FBI's Uniform Crime Reports estimated 9 million arrests during 1973. The Bureau says that 1,599,000 were for drunkenness. But several hundred thousand additional arrests for liquor-law violations, disorderly conduct, vagrancy, and panhandling were really for drunkenness. These figures do not include arrests for drunk driving, 946,800 of which occurred in 1973, according to the FBI's estimate.
2. Raymond T. Nimmer, *Two Million Unnecessary Arrests* (Chicago: American Bar Foundation, 1971), p. 86.
3. At the time it got started, I was director of the New York Civil Liberties Union. A representative of the Vera Foundation visited me to describe the

223

plan for the program. She said it would be compulsory, and I said that if it were, the NYCLU would challenge it in court. A few weeks later, she let me know the plan had been changed and it would be voluntary.

4. *Programs in Criminal Justice Reform* (New York: Vera Institute of Justice, 1972), p. 70.

5. Herbert Packer, *The Limits of the Criminal Sanction* (Stanford, Calif.: Stanford University Press, 1968), p. 347.

Chapter 3. Private Smokers

1. *From the Lands of the Scythians* (New York: The Metropolitan Museum of Art), 1975, p. 138. Reprinted from *The Persian Wars* (book IV) by Herodotus (New York: Random House, 1942).

2. David Musto, *The American Disease* (New Haven, Conn.: Yale University Press, 1973), p. 65.

3. The survey was conducted for the council by a Portland, Oregon, market-research firm, Bardsley and Haslacher, Inc., which interviewed 802 adults. The Drug Abuse Council was established by a consortium of private foundations in 1972.

4. The predecessor agency of the Bureau of Narcotics and Dangerous Drugs, which, after it in turn was discredited, gave way to the Drug Enforcement Administration. Before long, we should be getting yet another change of name in an effort to escape the odor of some of the recent scandals associated with the DEA.

5. Statement by the Drug Abuse Council, Washington, D.C., July 17, 1974.

6. Jay Cameron Hall, *Inside the Crime Lab* (Englewood Cliffs, N.J.: Prentice-Hall, 1970), p. 143.

Chapter 4. Drug Use: How the Law Creates Crime

1. The claim was made in 1966, a year Rockefeller had to run for reelection as governor. Rockefeller used it to justify his program for compulsory commitment of addicts. The program was abandoned as a failure a few years later, after New York had spent a billion dollars on it.

2. Irving Brant, *The Bill of Rights* (Indianapolis: Bobbs-Merrill, 1965), pp. 486–87.

3. The best account of the English experience is Horace Freeland Judson, *Heroin Addiction in Britain* (New York: Harcourt Brace Jovanovich, 1974).

4. Ibid., p. 139.
5. Edward M. Brecher and the Editors of *Consumer Reports, Licit and Illicit Drugs* (Boston: Little, Brown, 1972).
6. Ibid., p. 524.
7. Ibid., p. 532.

Chapter 5. Take Away All Guns

1. Robert Sherrill, *The Saturday Night Special* (Baltimore: Penguin, 1973), p. 319.
2. Irving Brant, *The Bill of Rights* (Indianapolis: Bobbs-Merrill, 1965), pp. 486–87.
3. Sherrill, *The Saturday Night Special*, p. 230.

Chapter 6. Police Crime: The Rotten Barrel

1. Albert J. Reiss, Jr., *The Police and the Public* (New Haven, Conn.: Yale University Press, 1971), pp. 156–62.
2. Ibid., p. 162.
3. Task Force Report, *The Police* (Washington, D.C.: U.S. Government Printing Office, 1967), pp. 120–43.
4. James Q. Wilson, *Varieties of Police Behavior* (Cambridge, Mass.: Harvard University Press, 1968), pp. 7–9.
5. Moreover, the Bureau notes that the arrest of one person may solve several crimes.
6. Other criminals also get caught. According to the FBI, about 80 percent of all murders, between 50 and 60 percent of all reported rapes, and between 60 and 70 percent of all aggravated assaults are cleared by arrests. Of these crimes, murder is the least likely to be repetitive, and therefore a very high proportion of arrests is necessary to be sure murderers are caught. Because rape and aggravated assault are more frequently repetitive crimes, the chances the perpetrators will be caught for one crime or another are at least as great as in the case of murderers.

Chapter 7. Random Law Enforcement: The Serendipity Theory

1. A guide to police explains how to tell if a person is suspicious. A sampling of its advice includes:

A. Be suspicious. This is a healthy police attitude, but it should be controlled and not too obvious.

B. Look for the unusual.
   1. Persons who do not "belong" where they are observed.
   2. Automobiles which do not "look right."

C. Subjects who should be subjected to field interrogations.
   1. Suspicious persons known to the officer from previous arrests, field interrogations, and observations. . . .
   2. Known trouble-makers near large gatherings.
   3. Persons who attempt to avoid or evade the officer.
   4. Exaggerated unconcern over contact with the officer.
   5. Visibly "rattled" when near the policeman.
   6. Unescorted women or young girls in public places, particularly at night in such places as cafes, bars, bus and train depots or street corners.

2. This is a reduction from 193,822,138 as of the end of 1972. The reduction resulted from a purge of prints received in connection with civilian national defense work in World War II, prints of all persons seventy-five years of age and older, and duplicates.

3. Of twelve known SLA members, six had been incinerated during a shootout with the Los Angeles police. Two were in prison in California for the murder of Oakland school superintendent Marcus Foster. The subsequent capture of Patricia Hearst, William Harris, and Emily Harris completed the roundup.

Chapter 8. Incorrigible Children

1. "Juvenile Delinquency Laws: Juvenile Women and the Double Standard of Morality," *UCLA Law Review* 19 (1971): 321–22.

2. Anthony Platt, *The Child Savers* (Chicago: University of Chicago Press, 1969), p. 76.

3. Task Force Report, *Juvenile Delinquency and Youth Crime* (Washington, D.C.: U.S. Government Printing Office, 1967), p. 3.

4. "They have no lawyers among them," Sir Thomas More said of his Utopia, "for they consider them as a sort of people whose profession it is to disguise matters." If there had been social workers in More's day, surely he would have excluded them, too, from his Utopia. It took the combined professional skills of lawyers and social workers to come up with the language of deception embracing all phases of the treatment of children accused of status offenses.

5. Task Force Report, *Juvenile Delinquency and Youth Crime*, p. 9304.

6. Marvin E. Wolfgang, Robert M. Figlio, and Thorsten Sellin, *Delinquency in a Birth Cohort* (Chicago: University of Chicago Press, 1972), p. 252.
7. *New York Times,* 7 May 1975.
8. Harriet Katz Berman, *The Privacy Report* (New York: ACLU Foundation, March 1975), p. 6.

Chapter 9. Public Responsibility for the Roots of Crime

1. Task Force Report, *Juvenile Delinquency and the Family: A Review and Discussion* (Washington, D.C.: U.S. Government Printing Office, 1967), pp. 188–221.
2. *New York Daily News,* 13 May 1975.
3. Brandt Allen and David W. Young, *Cost Barriers in Adoption* (The Colgate Darden Graduate School of Business Administration, University of Virginia, 1975).
4. At ages twelve and eleven, Larry and George are now genuinely hard to place. Predictably, they are expected to remain in foster care until they are eighteen and cost the city another $30,000 apiece. Or they might get sent to juvenile prisons, in which case the cost would be much higher.
5. *New York Times,* 5 April 1975.
6. See Joseph Goldstein, Anna Freud, and Albert J. Solnit, *Beyond the Best Interests of the Child* (New York: Free Press, 1973). The authors, all psychiatrists, argue that concern for continuity of relationships should be uppermost in child-placement decisions.

Chapter 10. Public Responsibility for the Roots of Crime: Continued

1. Blanche Bernstein and William Meegan, *The Impact of Welfare on Family Stability* (New York: Center for New York City Affairs, New School for Social Research, 1975), p. 103.

PART TWO: PUNISHMENT

Chapter 11. Recommended: A Double Standard

1. Marvin E. Frankel, *Criminal Sentences* (New York: Hill and Wang, 1973), p. 18.

2. Ramsey Clark, *Crime in America* (New York: Simon & Schuster, 1970).

3. Karl Menninger, *The Crime of Punishment* (New York: Viking, 1966), p. 261.

4. Quoted in David Rothman, *The Discovery of the Asylum* (Boston: Little, Brown, 1971), pp. 84–85.

5. David Rothman, "Behavior Modification in Total Institutions," *Hastings Center Report 5* (Hastings-on-Hudson, N.Y.: Hastings Center, 1975), p. 23.

6. Malcolm X, *The Autobiography of Malcolm X* (New York: Grove Press, 1966), p. 180.

7. Robert Martinson, "What Works?—Questions and Answers about Prison Reform," *The Public Interest,* Spring 1974, p. 49.

8. "Correctional Outcome: An Evaluation of 100 Reports," in Leon Radzinowicz and Marvin Wolfgang, eds., *Crime and Justice,* vol. 3 (New York: Basic Books, 1971).

9. C. S. Lewis, "The Humanitarian Theory of Punishment" in Joseph Goldstein, Alan M. Dershowitz, Richard D. Schwartz, eds., *Criminal Law* (New York: Free Press, 1974), pp. 713–714.

10. I can't help wondering whether this program at a Connecticut prison, intended as it is to get the prisoners interested in adult women, isn't really transforming pedophiles into rapists.

11. See Andrew von Hirsch, *Doing Justice,* to be published early in 1976 by Hill & Wang (New York) as the report of the Committee on the Study of Incarceration.

12. Norval Morris, *The Future of Imprisonment* (Chicago: University of Chicago Press, 1974), p. 66.

13. Ibid., p. 68.

14. Bruce J. Ennis and Thomas R. Litwack, "Psychiatry and the Presumption of Expertise: Flipping Coins in the Courtrooms," *California Law Review,* May 1974.

15. As distinguished from "specific deterrence." General deterrence aims at stopping others from committing crimes. Specific deterrence is aimed at stopping the criminal from repeating his crime for fear he will be punished again.

16. *New York Times,* 23 February 1975.

17. Norval Morris, *The Future of Imprisonment* (Chicago: University of Chicago Press, 1974), p. 79.

18. Gordon Tullock, "Does Punishment Deter Crime?," *The Public Interest,* Summer 1974, pp. 107–108.

19. C. S. Lewis, "The Humanitarian Theory of Punishment" in Joseph Goldstein, Alan M. Dershowitz, Richard D. Schwartz, eds., *Criminal Law* (New York: Free Press, 1974), p. 714.

20. James Fitzjames Stephen, the nineteenth-century historian of the criminal law of England, argued that a purpose "of coordinate importance" was to

give "definite expression and a solemn ratification and justification to the hatred which is excited by the commission of the offence."

21. Somewhat inconsistently, I believe, the Committee on the Study of Incarceration embraces differing punishments for people previously convicted of crime along with its adherence to commensurate deserts.

Chapter 12. Plea Bargaining: The Need for Reform

1. Henry T. Lummus in "The Trial Judge," 1937, quoted in Joseph Goldstein, Alan M. Dershowitz, Richard D. Schwartz, eds., *Criminal Law* (New York: Free Press, 1974), pp. 45–46.

Chapter 13. Unexplained and Unfair Sentencing

1. Friedrich Nietzsche, *Genealogy of Morals*, trans. Francis Golffing (Garden City, N.Y.: Doubleday, 1956), pp. 212–13.
2. Willard Gaylin, *Partial Justice* (New York: Knopf, 1974).
3. James V. Bennett, *I Chose Prison* (New York: Knopf, 1970).

Chapter 14. Prison and Alternatives

1. They should get the minimum wage while performing public-service work. Most criminals would need it to survive.
2. Herbert Packer, *The Limits of the Criminal Sanction* (Stanford, Calif.: Stanford University Press, 1968), p. 273.
3. William E. Cockerham, "Behavior Modification for Child Molesters," *Corrections Magazine*, Vol. 1, No. 3, January-February 1975, p. 78.
4. Ibid., pp. 79–80. The reader will recall it was rats in Room 101 in George Orwell's *Nineteen Eighty-four*. There, too, each person was tortured in whatever way he feared most.
5. Jessica Mitford, *Kind and Usual Punishment* (New York: Knopf, 1973). The Food and Drug Administration requires that new drugs be tested on human beings before being marketed. This makes the drug companies very eager for cheap and willing human subjects.
6. David Wexler, "Therapeutic Justice," *Minnesota Law Review* 57 (1973): 289.
7. Erving Goffman, *Asylums* (Garden City, N.Y.: Doubleday Anchor, 1961).
8. Erving Goffman, *Symposium on Preventive and Social Psychiatry* (Washington, D.C.: Walter Reed Army Institute of Research, 1958), p. 46.

9. Norval Morris, *The Future of Imprisonment* (Chicago: University of Chicago Press, 1974), pp. 85–121.
10. Ibid., pp. 108–109.

Chapter 15. Eliminate Parole and God Playing

1. This figure excludes the jail population. It numbers about 160,000.
2. Alvin Bronstein, "Rules for Playing God," *The Civil Liberties Review*, Vol. 1, No. 3, Summer 1974, p. 119.
3. Murder, assault, and rape are rarely crimes of Federal prisoners and do not figure in the listing.
4. David Rudenstine, *Prison Without Walls: Report on New York Parole* (New York: Praeger, 1975).
5. A prison psychiatrist serves the institution, not the prisoner. Unlike other psychiatrists, he does not necessarily feel any obligation to maintain confidential what his patient tells him.
6. Rudenstine, *Prison Without Walls*, p. 46.
7. William R. Coons, *Attica Diary* (New York: Stein and Day, 1972), pp. 219–20.
8. George Jackson, *Soledad Brother: The Prison Letters of George Jackson* (New York: Bantam, 1970), p. 161.
9. J. Jack Griswold, Mike Misenheimer, Art Powers, and Ed Tromanhauser, *An Eye for an Eye* (New York: Pocket Books, 1971), p. 53.
10. Jessica Mitford, *Kind and Usual Punishment* (New York: Knopf, 1973), p. 92.
11. James V. Bennett, *I Chose Prison* (New York: Knopf, 1970), p. 187.
12. Ibid., p. 188.
13. Norval Morris, *The Future of Imprisonment* (Chicago: University of Chicago Press, 1974), p. 37.
14. Ibid.
15. Ibid., pp. 35–36.
16. Ronald Goldfarb and Linda Singer, *After Conviction: A Review of the American Correctional System* (New York: Simon & Schuster, 1973), p. 278.
17. Rudenstine, *Prison Without Walls*, p. 166.
18. American Friends Service Committee, *Struggle for Justice* (New York: Hill & Wang, 1971), p. 148.
19. *Attica: The Official Report of the New York State Commission on Attica* (New York: Bantam, 1972), p. 93.

Chapter 16. Stigma

1. Aryeh Neier, *Dossier: The Secret Files They Keep on You* (New York: Stein and Day, 1975).
2. One man in every two and one woman in every eight in the United States acquire arrest records at some time in their lives. Because people try to conceal their arrest records, however, they don't have a sense of identification with others similarly afflicted.

Chapter 17. Summing Up

1. James Q. Wilson, *Thinking About Crime* (New York: Basic Books, 1975), p. 96.

Index

345.73   Neier, Aryeh
N397c   Crime & punishment: a radical
           solution

DATE DUE

AP 27'76

DISCARDED

GAYLORD   PRINTED IN U.S.A.